Toxic Cultures

How to recognize, evaluate
and fix them

By
Nick A. Shepherd

Jannas Publications

An EduVision Inc. Knowledge Service

Corporate Culture

ISBN 978-1-7781309-3-9

Cover design by: EduVision Inc.
Author: Nick A. Shepherd
FCPA., FCGA., FCCA., FCMC

Jannas Publications
Division of Eduvision Inc.
Ottawa, Canada.

Dedication

This book is dedicated to all those who are working to change and improve the behaviour of business organizations globally.

This includes the inspirational and dedicated leaders that have realized that "there is a better way" and are trying to make the changes required. It is also dedicated to all those members of the workforce, who are increasingly becoming vocal about the need for organizations to be more people centric. It is dedicated to all those individuals, both volunteers and compensated, who are providing help, guidance, support, and ideas to leaders about how they might approach implementing sustainable change.

Of course, it is dedicated to my wonderful wife who has the patience of a saint, with a husband who just always seems to have "stuff to do."

Corporate Culture

Contents

Corporate Culture

Corporate Culture

Foreword

In 2022, the "Great Resignation" is a popular topic. Following a challenging period of dealing with COVID, many people are faced with returning to work. But there is a problem. Between April and September 2021, a record number of more than 24 million American employees left their jobs. In many nations where a large percentage of people worked from home, the same situation has developed[i].

Business leaders are struggling to respond to the factors driving the mass exodus. Additionally, they are looking for ways to hold on to valued employees. At the same time, the press continues to report scandals and stories related to toxic workplaces, related to organizations and the people that work there.

Workplaces that exhibit discrimination, lack of inclusiveness, disrespect, unethical practices, and abuse. Where sexual and other harassment exists often committed by owners, managers, and others in leadership roles. Where employees feel that they are bullied and taken advantage of. Where unreasonable and unfair work practices exist. Where hiring and promotion are often based on favouritism. Many of these are illegal – all are socially unacceptable – yet all seem to be part of the way that organizations are run.

Then there are other relationship problems. Cliques that develop and gossip that pervades the workplace. People who fail to communicate with others. Those who work in silos and fail to cooperate and collaborate.

All of these problems either create or contribute to a toxic workplace. A place where people go to "earn their living" but would really rather not be there. Where the feeling is often "that's just the way it is." Where any efforts to raise the problems are either ignored, or if raised, become the source of fear of reprisals. Where people keep quiet – just keep their heads down and do the job.

A recent study[ii] reveals that although many employers seem to think that compensation is a key issue in solving the "back to work" problem – in fact the largest issue is the corporate culture. While this may vary across industries, the reality is that across the board, the highest consistent correlation for employee turnover is the culture.

Leaders seem to believe that employee engagement is the same thing as culture. No. Employee engagement is one of the many outcomes from an effective work culture. Trying to fix engagement without building it on a solid foundation of culture will fail. Leaders create "the crucible" within which work takes place. The business model that brings together all the required resources, to execute business plans. Culture is a leadership issue.

Workplace culture permeates every single aspect of a business operation. Creating a positive culture is strategic. If success is to be achieved, culture must be strategically positioned at an equivalent level to business purpose.

This book is designed to complement my other two books on corporate culture[iii], and to focus on the underlying link between strategy, leadership, and a positive workplace. Avoiding a toxic culture is essential to sustain an organizations brand and reputation. To eliminate financial and market surprises from unplanned events. But also, to help minimize employee turnover. To better attract and retain the talented people needed. To create a competitive advantage through applying people's enthusiasm for change, innovation, and creativity. To develop and retain the intellectual capital needed in a knowledge economy.

Corporate Culture

Most of all, to address societies need for responsible business. Business that contributes to economic success by attracting investment and delivering growth, value, profits, and dividends. Business that is seen as a valued member of society through its support and commitment to people. By creating work places where health and safety extend to broad based well-being. Where stress and mental health issues are understood and guarded against.

Where people want to return to work. Where they see their work as personally fulfilling but also want to interact with others in the workplace, because it's a positive experience. Where there is emotional and social satisfaction, but also where their ideas are stimulated and grown through interacting with others.

Let's outlaw toxic workplaces. Let's deliver leadership at its' best.

Nick Shepherd
Ottawa, September 2022

Corporate Culture

1 Introduction

Toxic cultures are destroying organizations and personal relationships. They eat away at human patience and endurance and diminish human potential, creativity, and innovation. No matter whether in business, or in sports, in personal or professional relationships toxic cultures need to be minimized, and where possible eliminated.

Whose job is it to make that happen? Everyone's. As individuals we need to think about and improve relationships with each other. As leaders we need to stamp out behaviours that diminish the individual. Are we to be seen as builders of human possibility and potential, or as demolition experts? There is a choice. Business as usual – or a realization that whatever we do, ultimately we are "all in this together."

Toxic cultures are a topical issue, but they are not new. Human beings have always experienced toxic relationships – at work, at home and in society generally. This book will focus on toxic cultures in organizations.

The foundation of toxic cultures is poor human behaviour. So, this book is about human behaviour, but is also about leadership, because the types of behaviour that lead to toxic cultures are impacted by effective leaders.

This book is important because a growing number of corporate and organizational issues are being traced back to organizational culture. Most recently, the "great resignation" has been occurring as people who have spent up to two years working at home, no longer want to return to the office. Why?

Because in many organizations returning to "the office" not only requires the frustrations of commuting but involves being "forced" to spend time with people who make them uncomfortable. How does being uncomfortable in a work situation manifest itself? Discrimination. Abuse. Harassment. Demeaning and snide remarks. Lack of fair treatment. Many people have realized they can still get their job done but live a much less stressful life. Who would want to go back there?

Everyone can take lessons from discussions in this book. For those in leadership positions, it should help provide a wake-up call to respond to the real changes that need to be made in their organizations. For others it should offer some opportunity for personal reflection and possible opportunities to improve how we interact with one another.

Why did I write this? Because I have a passion for building a better society where we treat each other with more respect. I know toxic relationships. My father was a violent alcoholic that my mother suffered with until leaving when I was about thirteen. I witnessed aggressive behaviour if you didn't "fit in" at a private boarding school in England; I was subjected to and observed bullying. I walked out on my first boss who was prone to violent verbal outbursts, together with clouds of spittle.

I have also been an initiator of violence – allowing psychological and emotional issues to "overpower control" and inflict (mostly psychological) damage on others. And yes, those sorts of outburst can be the drivers of growing mental health issues. I have worked in businesses where I observed unbelievable bad behaviour and also visited many companies in my consulting career where I observed how poorly some people were treated. I have played an active role in professional organizations globally and again observed how different national backgrounds impact behaviour and how, in any culture, negative personal behaviour can impact the effectiveness of the whole diverse group.

But I have also observed the opposite – organizations of all types where people are thriving, and leaders clearly work to create and sustain an atmosphere for human achievement. Organizations that successfully attract people and retain talent – because the people WANT to be there – to be part of the group. Relationships that are happy and fulfilling. I know it IS possible and it does happen.

I have also attended many seminars, workshops and courses over my career dealing with human aspects of work life. I have read a lot of books about personal development and psychology and have been able to put these into practice. I have had a life long journey of interacting with other people during which I have tried to learn about what works best in building relationships. I have been married for over fifty years which is one of life's greatest lessons in relationship development. Additionally, we brought up three children including those "teenage years" when all sorts of behavioural challenges take place! Following that, I was able to watch a daughter become a parent and give birth to, nurture and help develop their own three children. I was able to watch and compare her approaches to relationship building from a different perspective than my own.

We are often told by the "professionals" to "take control." We are encouraged to "leave emotion out of it" and that "there is no place for emotion in business"- (especially in business!). We are also taught that in dealing with these sorts of problems in society, that we should "not take it personally" and to "suck it up." We are also told that if someone else says something that makes us feel demeaned or diminished, that is their problem, and we should have enough strength to just ignore it. We should be strong enough to just shrug it off. Many of us grow up in a society where men especially are taught to control their emotions, and that any sign of an emotional response is a sign of weakness. We even go so far as buying into the misguided theories that rapists cannot be fully blamed for their actions if they were attracted to the woman or if she was wearing provocative clothing. I'm sorry this is all bullshit. (Sorry about that).

Claiming to not be responsible for your own behaviour is a cop-out. While I agree that we should do our best to not get too weighed down by the poor behaviours of others – especially when directed at us, this in no way relieves the perpetrator of the poor behaviour as innocent. A key part of developing as human beings is to understand and control emotions – NOT to eliminate them. We ALL have a responsibility to think about how our own behaviour impacts others. If we fail to take responsibility for that, we fail to grow as a member of civilized society. We, each of us, has a MAJOR role to play in the success or failure of our fellow human beings.

Hope the passion is coming through? No one is immune from this. We all exist with some type of relationships in our lives. They go from the simple "one on one" of a couple living together (and we all know that even with just two people involved how hard that can be). At the other end of the scale are organizations and societies where the goal is to all get along as best we can for the betterment of every member of the group.

Relationship issues are everywhere. A CEO who has problems with her board, or at home with the family, or with members of her leadership team. An employee who has issues with fellow employees, or their supervisor, or with their union. A wife who has issues at the soccer club with other parents when she takes the children. A woman enjoying a quiet drink after work with a colleague, only to be subjected to remarks and innuendoes. Road rage when we least expect it. This is because above all else, we are human. There is a lot of opportunity for improvement.

If you are a leader at any level, your goal should be to strive to make the workplace an attractive, encouraging, and supportive place to be. Somewhere that people actually look forward to being part of. After all, as a leader you create the "crucible" within which human potential is brought together for the greater good.

As an individual, try to reflect on how you interact with others. If you need to say something consider first whether to actually open your mouth at all. If it is necessary and adds value, think about how it might be heard and interpreted by others. Take care in what you say and how you act. Also feel free to tell others how you feel, if something happens that seems unacceptable to you. But do it in a non-threatening way. Overall, my hope is that through reading this book we all become more aware of the power that we have to build others up and create a better world or to continue the demolition process and the slide to human mediocrity.

For all of us – listen. Listen to what people say. Try and discover their feelings through observation or asking. We live in a world of sounds bites. Of course, we are listening – but are we really hearing?

Corporate Culture

2 What is a toxic culture?

The term toxic workplace is being increasingly seen in the press and linked to "people issues" from discontent and low "engagement," to legal action. While more visible in the western world where democracy is supposed to underpin capitalism, the reality is that it happens everywhere people are brought together. The timing of this book is interesting. A new author just released a book titled "Bully Market: My Story of Money and Misogyny at Goldman Sachs" – kind of topical.

In the US, video game company Activision Blizzard is being sued by the California Department of Fair Employment and Housing for charges related to fostering a toxic culture within the company. The allegations include bullying, sexual harassment, and racial discrimination. Female employees on the product team "World of Warcraft" allege non-consensual physical contact, unwanted advances, and demeaning comments including "jokes about rape." The suit comes on the heels of a two-year investigation into the company's toxic environment. It also resulted in the first time in history that the SEC has raised the issue of "nondisclosed material factors" in a public organizations annual compliance reporting – related to non-financial requirements but to underlying "material issues" related to people.

In Canada, allegations of a toxic work culture underpin the abrupt firing of CTV anchor Lisa LaFlamme. According to the Globe and Mail newspaper, "in the past three years there have been at least three formal reviews involving Bell Media newsrooms, in response to complaints over incidents that included alleged bullying by managers, sexual harassment, and the use of the N-word during an inclusive-leadership training session." A significant public outcry followed the firing, resulting in the "suspension pending an investigation" of the responsible senior executive. According to the Globe and Mail, staff members say they are "apprehensive that the process will not lead to substantial change – because, they say, past reviews didn't either." This would seem to suggest a problem culture.

In the UK a recent example of toxic workplace culture allegations, was at an innovative and creative brewing company named BrewDog, based in Aberdeen. The company had been incredibly successful initially in its home market and then internationally. The CEO and co-founder, James Watt was at the centre of a whirlwind of accusations of a toxic and sexist workplace culture, that "exploded" when Punks with Purpose, a group of 300 former and current workers, signed a letter complaining of a policy of "growth at all costs".

The group alleged that this involved "cutting corners on health and safety, espousing values it did not live by, and creating a "toxic" culture that left staff suffering from mental illness." In a subsequent BBC documentary James Watt hotly denied allegations of predatory behaviour. There has been some "back-peddling," and the company has since taken a number of steps to address the issue. Time will tell but in the early years, the founder developed a reputation of pushing back against any sort of regulation or control.

There are many examples in these three countries. Looking at recent headlines include allegations of toxic workplaces at Amazon, Tesla, Mattel, and Wal Mart. Even television shows are not immune – newsrooms are famous for culture issues and the Ellen DeGeneres show was found to have poor practices and there are examples of NBC having problems. Ellen DeGeneres was apparently unaware of many of the issues – similar to the responses of many leaders when these problems come to the surface. Clearly they all start with allegations. Some are eventually proven to be isolated examples; others are larger issues. Some will require "major surgery" to correct, some may lead to legal challenges. Some may be dismissed as "spurious." However, there are enough examples to suggest there is a problem. Additional ideas and detail are provided by several mini-case studies in chapter 4 "A deeper dive into toxic culture."

Some may remember the business and financial failure of Carillion a major UK public company. Comments from a Parliamentary committee[iv] investigating later included comments such as, "Carillion's board presided over a rotten corporate culture and was both responsible and culpable for its catastrophic demise." "The report is highly critical of the corporate culture that led to Carillion's collapse."

Forbes refers to toxic workplaces as "cultures that are rife with hostility, cliques, gossip, mistrust, and selfishness." Another author refers to a study conducted anonymously which suggested that a toxic culture was "non-inclusive, where members across gender, race, sexual identity and orientation, disability and age don't feel they are treated fairly, welcomed or included in key decisions." Yet another blog refers to a toxic workplace "where the workplace is plagued by fighting, drama and unhappy employees."

Extracts from a 2021 article on toxic workplaces from HRPA[v] quotes Professor G. Richard Shell, award-winning scholar, Chair of the Wharton School's Legal Studies, and Business Ethics Department, who suggests that *"when a workplace is truly toxic, dysfunction is the organizational norm and mean-spirited behaviour occurs daily. The dominant daily emotion among employees is anxiety. They fear that they will be bullied, humiliated and/or shamed into silent compliance with values they reject. People in hostile working environments feel psychologically unsafe, as employers often violate workers' human rights, health, and safety rights and/or rights against constructive dismissal."*

Notice that in almost every situation these toxic and poor culture allegations rest on individual or collective human behavior. No matter at what level or in what business. One can be sure of at least three outcomes of toxic cultures:

- They will permeate the whole organization if not resolved.
- They will impact both internal and external relationships – including those with clients and customers.
- When they occur they will reduce employee commitment which will show up in either hidden or visible productivity problems.

No one is immune from the risk of a toxic culture because people come together in groups. When this is to achieve a common and shared purpose, then the better the environment for cooperation and collaboration, the more successful the "collective" will be. This is true for business – profit and not-for-profit, public, and private, large, or small, government – local, municipal, regional, state, provincial, national. It is true in family groups, from a partnership of two people to a clan or dynasty spreading over generations and locations.

The impact that the behaviour of large corporations has on people around the world is major. With the growth of companies like Facebook, Apple, Amazon, Alphabet / Google, and Netflix[vi], the decisions that leaders make related to corporate behaviour, impacts people in almost every country around the world. Counting employees is totally inadequate as much activity is now undertaken by suppliers and other third parties. These companies are influential in impacting social norms around the world, both internally and externally.

The greater stress that people are placed under, the greater the risk for a toxic culture developing. In a competitive world, where the drive to compete and succeed is often paramount, the risk of a toxic culture developing will increase. The larger the group, the more challenging it will be to sustain a positive culture, and spot and resolve cultural risk issues at the operational level.

Add to this mix the multi-cultural make up of many workforces, plus the differing generations trying to work together, plus the reality of operating globally for many organizations and the risk increases yet again. Finally, the evolution of the knowledge economy that requires a higher level of interaction between individuals, and we have a business challenge that has come of age.

Toxic culture lies at the very heart of many apparent organizational challenges being seen today. If the call for "renewed capitalism" or "stakeholder capitalism" or "responsible business" are to result in refreshment and renewal, the foundation will have to be focusing on culture in the workplace (as a minimum!).

This was predicted. In their 1998 book, "The Centreless Corporation[vii]," the authors identified the changes that were occurring in business and focused a chapter on the triumph of people power. They identified that people would be one of three driving competitive advantages, and they focused on the changing relationships between the company and its people. They identified a new people partnership that would meet the following needs:

1. Continually improve performance and enhance value to shareholders.
2. Enable the company to attract and retain top talent.
3. Motivate all employees to work to their fullest potential.
4. Develop the skills of both blue and white collar workers.
5. Balance the interests of ALL stakeholders, including shareholders, employees, unions, government, and society.

Most of these stated needs for the new relationship are often quoted today as issues related to people management and leadership. Not a word about culture, but a great deal of talk about shared values. Who was to realize that this was what they were talking about. The culture.

3 The impact of toxic culture

The previous chapter includes aspects that demonstrate one of the important impacts from a toxic culture – poor publicity. But it is far deeper than that. One of the current trends in management is a focus on employee engagement. Some of the more solid linkages between engagement and positive outcomes comes from the annual Gallup Q12 Meta-Analysis reports[viii]. Their latest report clearly demonstrates a positive correlation between employee engagement and a "basket" of organizational outcome measures.

But how does this connect to culture? Is good employee engagement an outcome of a positive culture? Is culture synonymous with engagement? The challenge for management is the search for cause and effect relationships. Experts point to many things that organizations need to do in order to improve employee engagement; one is left feeling that doing these things will, de facto, lead to a positive culture. Sadly, that is not true. There are many organizations out there, implementing many of the things necessary to enhance engagement yet many still struggle to avoid the surprises that come from a poor culture. It is like a virus.

The goal of a culture that is strong enough to create a strategic competitive advantage, is to optimize the total integrated performance of the organization as a whole. The challenge for many leaders is that a poor or toxic culture only shows up when something major goes wrong. But what if one could look for symptoms of a poor culture – some that are affecting performance but have not yet reached the critical level, and try and monitor these as early warning signs?

My earlier book "The Cost of Poor Culture[ix]," discussed three specific aspects of cost, where poor culture will impact performance. The problem is that in almost all situations, current financial reporting does a poor job of highlighting such risks, and when they are reflected, it often occurs after the event. These risks are:

- **Financial surprises** Unanticipated impacts on financial performance that occur due to control failures and unanticipated behavior (examples would be legal and regulatory fines and penalties, as well as negative impacts in areas such as brand and reputation).
- **Buried costs** The impacts of lower or poor financial performance that come from restraints on value creation, which result in lower output, higher costs, lower revenues and lower quality of products and services.
- **Lost opportunities** from collaboration and cooperation – people applying their talents, to enhance value, increase output, lower costs, increase revenues and enhance quality.

3.1   Financial surprises

Financial surprises are typically unanticipated, have a negative impact on earnings, and will usually reduce organizational value. The failure of Carillion probably came as a surprise to many of the company directors. Likewise major financial scandals also come as surprises. Many readers will remember the Wells Fargo bank scandal. In the banks drive to enhance profitability, phantom accounts were opened by bank staff, and unauthorized loans approved. The financial meltdown in 2008 – 2010 was also a surprise. Why did people do these things? What led them to believe it was right and necessary let alone legal or ethical?

For business, unplanned surprises often come in the form of fines and penalties. Looking at fines and penalties imposed in the US between 2000 and 2020, the top ten contains eight banks or financial institutions. Their collective fines and penalties were $230 billion, yes billion. Were these surprises or the cost of known, calculated decisions by senior leadership? Clearly some people think the failings related to culture. The New York Federal Reserve[x] has been focusing research, and training and development on the impact of culture within a governance context in the financial sector. They certainly see a connection.

3.2   Buried costs

In the second situation, impacts caused by "sub-optimization" are often not visible, as the higher operating costs lie buried within the existing expenses. While performance benchmarking might indicate an opportunity for improvement, the excess costs are not clearly reported by the organization or understood by management – it's just "what it is."

Often, as a result of these perceived excess costs, organizations resort to short-term cost-cutting measures like layoffs, which might have short-term benefits but, in the longer term, do little to enhance cultural maturity; such measures deplete intangible value, often causing deterioration in employee morale and other areas such as client and supplier relationships. These then further reduce morale and motivation to create a "vicious circle." Ultimately, they destroy value (and people).

However, these buried costs can sometimes show up in non-financial indicators such as numbers of grievances filed; numbers of disciplinary actions; disputes; complaints filed for diversity or discrimination; health and safety violations and statistics; higher (voluntary) employee turnover; turnover of key / critical positions; number of staff not completing probationary period; results of employee feedback / surveys; percentage of positions filled internally. Every one of these drives up operating costs and drives down morale and engagement. However, many are not widely reported, and the monetary impact is often buried.

3.3 Lost opportunities

The third area - lost opportunity, is the most strategically critical. Most organizations develop performance improvement budgets but rarely is the question asked, - how much better could performance be if everything and everyone was operating as a fully effective, aligned, and holistic system? The foundation of a successful understanding of the holistic nature of culture can start with an understanding a few foundational points.

1. Organizations – especially businesses, tend to be TASK focused. Driven by their "raison d'être" – often referred to as their purpose.
2. Every organization develops its own unique business model, which brings together the key resources required to operate. (This was traditionally referred to as "men, money and machines" but more recently as the six key capitals – financial, natural, manufactured, human, relationships and social, and intellectual).
3. People have always been a key component of the required resources.
4. People are multi-dimensional; like machines they utilize logic, but unlike machines, people can also be strongly driven by emotion.

The first foundation can often be the Achilles heel of recognizing culture issues. As long as an organization is focused on task and delivering acceptable performance "what lies beneath the surface" seems less important. The watchword being kudo's to the CEO, board, and leader that "achieves success." This problem and its potential impact were best epitomized in the success days of General Electric during a review of recognition and reward of supervisors.

The company developed a four quadrant grid within which managerial performance was positioned. There had been growing concern that while compensation as well as promotion, were heavily weighted to "task output / results" – getting the job done, there were some undesirable side effects that were strategically impacting the organizations development of human potential and, as a result having a negative impact on enterprise sustainability and succession. The grid looked something like this:

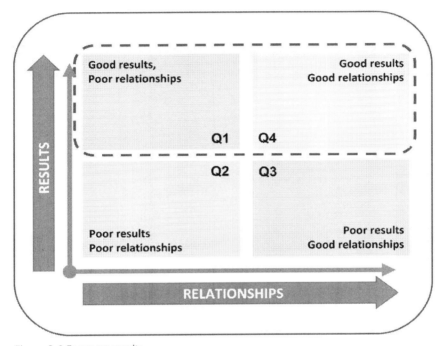

Figure 3-1 Focus on results

The two boxes marked Q1 and Q4 were the focus of compensation and performance for managers. After all, they were achieving their task – delivering on their goals and objectives which mainly dealt with outcomes and outputs. Treating these two boxes equally took no account on "how" the manager delivered the results; some managers were able to develop excellent "engagement" based on good relationships with key staff (and other stakeholder resources) and were in Q4, but others focused solely on "getting the job done" and were in Q1.

The impact was interesting when the people involved in reviewing the effectiveness of the compensation and incentive system started to look at

BOTH getting the job done, and the human impact from the way in which the results were achieved. Here are the words used about managers in each quadrant.

"Managers whose performance was in Q4 – not only deliver on performance commitments but believe in and further GE's small company values. These are the "A" players who will represent the core of the future leadership into the next century.

Managers whose performance was in Q1 – these managers make the numbers but don't share our values. Assessing performance of these managers is the most difficult of all – they deliver results but <u>"...they do it while ignoring values. They are a destructive force because they poison the environment, wear people down, stifle creativity and cause valuable talent down the line to flee GE."</u>

Managers whose performance was in Q3 – these managers believe and lead using our values but sometimes miss their commitments. These managers need to be coached, encouraged, and given another chance. (Clearly their relationships with their people are positive – but "intent" has not resulted in the desired "outcomes).

Finally, those managers who are assessed as performing in Q2 – these managers do not meet commitments and nor do they share our values. They will not last long at GE."

Note that there are two key points. Q4 managers, differ from Q1 managers as they are clearly "keepers." Essential for the future and sustainability of the business. CRITICAL talent that the organization wants to keep. People that the organization has clearly invested in who are delivering what is needed. A positive culture is strategically important in motivating and retaining key people.

The second point (Q1) is even more critical – and bears repeating –

"They are a destructive force because they poison the environment, wear people down, stifle creativity and cause valuable talent down the line to flee GE."

If one wanted to see the impact of a poor culture of both engagement and performance, here is the evidence from an organization who clearly saw a strategic disconnect if managers operated in Q1. But the challenge in making any change is that our thinking is SO task oriented that we tend to "short-change" the human impacts.

It is this last aspect that culture focuses on. Culture is about "behaviour" – it's about "the way we do things around here." As such, unlike most other resources or capitals, effective utilization requires addressing both the task component – what people do, but also the emotional or relationship component. This leads us to one of the most critical aspects of the impact of a poor, especially toxic culture.

That is the impact on the individual both within and outside the workplace. The impact related to cost borne not just by the employer but by society as a whole. The rise in mental health issues, and the calls for "re-humanizing the workplace" come from a growing concern that the way businesses operate today is having a negative impact on society. A wise leader knows this and also knows that solving the problem for society will also enhance the work environment, leading to performance improvement.

A study published in the MITSloan Management Review in early 2022[xi], reported that "a toxic corporate culture, for example, is 10.4 times more powerful than compensation in predicting a company's attrition rate compared with its industry."

The Society of Human Resources Management (SHRM), the leading USA HR society, estimates that toxic cultures cost business more than $44 billion per year – even prior to the Great Resignation.

An April 2022 report by Deloitte UK[xii] related to sickness and mental health in the workplace, estimates that it costs the UK economy over £100 billion and the government specifically about £50 billion in terms of lost revenues and added expenses.

The case is clear. There are solid business reasons for addressing a toxic culture. While the real costs may be hidden, lying buried somewhere in the financial statements, the actual impact on the business, the people and society is major.

Organizations can benefit from eliminating toxic culture, and in doing so they can have a significant societal impact. These dual benefits are at the heart of the need for change and the call for "responsible business."

4 Deeper dive into toxic culture

Somehow many of us have in our mind a knowledge that the problem exists. In the age of global communications and social media the story pops up, people comment, editorials are written and sadly we move on without any real changes being made. When society shifts in terms of opinions and levels of acceptable behaviour, then this should drive real change.

Many organizations respond to issues, problems, and scandals but with "the quick fix." People are disciplined or fired. Some training courses are set in place. The issue becomes the subject of a town hall meeting and maybe a more in depth program is put in place – but are these real changes or "window dressing?" Knee jerk reactions rather than thought through, serious in-depth changes to the way an organization operates?

In the next few pages, a number of situations will be presented that have occurred and the details of which have been made public. In some cases, these situations remain as un-proven allegations, in others a legal case or investigation has been conducted and a verdict has been delivered. The goal of presenting each situation is to both remind readers of real life situations that have taken place, and to illustrate some of the behaviours that are behind toxic cultures.

It must be emphasised that these are not some sort of devil oriented organizations – bad places where only bad things happen. Many are trying to do a good job. The majority of people who work in them are probably good people. The CEO may even be a good, well-motivated and sincere individual. The problem is that somehow, somewhere, things went "off track." These serve as illustrations of how great a challenge running an organization is – especially a large one. Especially worrying is that often the CEO or senior management is totally unaware of the problem.

Each organization was established with a clear social purpose to serve society as a vehicle for economic activity. Each also has an organizational purpose – to provide a needed product or service – or to develop and provide new and innovative offerings that consumers would embrace once available.

Each illustrates that when even the smallest problem occurs it can have major consequences. For some organizations, the culture supports "problems waiting to happen" for others they might be able to honestly claim that this was an aberration – an exception. The key issue is that managing culture is all about managing behavioural risk.

These examples are important as they illustrate how pervasive behavioural issues are. In all cases, management decision making, and leadership behaviour impacted "the way we do things around here." By so doing, all of these actions did, in some way or another impact the organizational culture.

Beliefs and values drive decision making. The impact of decisions is the reality that people inside and outside an organizations observe and are personally and directly impacted by. This is how culture is created, sustained, or destroyed.

(Note that in the cases that follow, some footnotes have been added as there are also large numbers of articles and commentaries available for the reader to access independently).

4.1   The Witches Hat

The headline reads *"Banker wins £2m for sexual discrimination in the "witches hat" case."* The settlement was awarded in 2022 by a panel in London, but the offences went back several years. It was a classic case involving pay discrimination, victimization, harassment, and demeaning behaviour, topped off by a drunken colleague leaving a witches hat on the persons desk when she was away at lunch. This was no junior employee – Stacey Macken was a £120, 000 a year finance specialist.

After being hired Stacey realized that she was being paid less than males doing the same job. She was ridiculed by people using the phrase "not now Stacey." Her bosses were said to have acted "spitefully and vindictively."

What does this settlement tell us about the culture? The same bank has also settled a case in the USA on violation of sanctions at a cost of $8.9 billion. They settled for $40 million after a Jewish employee claimed he was penalized for complaining about having to watch a video that depicted Hitler as a rival bank. The company was ordered to pay $115 million in 2015 for price rigging.

One could conclude that **this bank has a toxic work culture** where internal behaviour does not reflect generally accepted "norms." Maybe today – some years later, it has improved things? Where was leadership? Was this behaviour supported or just ignored as "this is the way it is" or "boys will be boys?" Maybe they thought they were just having some harmless fun? It is worrying that this sort of problem seems to occur in high-paying industries.

4.2   The "frat house"

In 2021 after a two year inquiry by the California Department of Fair Employment and Housing, charges were laid against Activision Blizzard, a major California company, who is a leader in the world of computer gaming software. These charges allege that the company ran a "frat boy" culture; discriminated against female employees in terms and conditions of employment, work assignments, promotion, and termination. The agency stated that *"company leadership consistently failed to take steps to prevent discrimination, harassment and retaliation."*

The SEC was concerned enough to open the first ever investigation into Activision's annual security filings based on the materiality of human relationships and their impact on investors. These investigations are continuing. The company also opened an investigation and as a result dozens were fired or disciplined. A board investigation concluded that these were isolated incidents. The company settled a similar lawsuit brought by the Federal government. The company has also been accused of intimidation and union busting.

The company is now in the process of being purchased by Microsoft, whose CEO has stated that *"the success of Microsoft's biggest deal ever rides on rehabilitating Activision Blizzards culture."*

Investigations and lawsuits continue but the board of Activision concluded that there was not a leadership issue. They recently re-appointed the CEO, who is alleged to have known about these issues, that date back to 2017 or 2018. This will be an interesting case to watch as it moves forward. Certainly, Microsoft thinks there is a problem.

4.3   In the public eye

When you are already "in the public's eye" the risk of problems and scandals emerging is higher. The BBC, as a well known, UK based global broadcaster is more vulnerable than most to allegations of a poor culture. Around 2012, the BBC was suddenly hit with a series of scandals when it was revealed that some of its key "talent" had been involved in the sexual abuse of children. Most famous of these were Jimmy Saville, Rolf Harris, and Stuart Hall. Although these cases dated back decades, the organization was accused on "knowing about but ignoring" the problems.

Although the BBC is very diligent about its' culture including employment practices, a 2018 incident demonstrated the challenge. Allegations of unfair pay and the resulting resignation of the head of the China bureau resulted in an independent enquiry. While the results indicated that the BBC had the right policies and procedures in place, is suggested that there remained room for improvement. A 2020 report by the Equality and Human Rights Commission[xiii] included the following:

"We found that in two-thirds of the cases we reviewed the BBC had not communicated its consideration of equal pay clearly to the employees concerned at the informal stage. This left some employees in doubt about whether equal pay had been considered or not. The BBC has been slow to resolve complaints, and its use of independent experts did not meet the level of independence and objectivity that some staff had expected. Grievance processes can be stressful in any organisation. During the investigation, we heard from some women who told us the stress and anxiety brought about by the grievance process had a damaging effect on their health."

A clear reflection that of the importance of culture – rather than just focusing on policy and procedure. Communications, empathy, listening.

4.4   The wild west

There was a major scandal about creating false accounts at Wells Fargo Bank, that was discovered in about 2017. The bank settled for $3 billion and admitted that *"it had pressured employees to meet unrealistic sales goals, that led thousands of employees to provide millions of accounts or (other) products to customers under false pretences or without consent, often by creating false records or misusing customers identities."*

The bank has also been accused of holding fake interviews for staff – even after a position has been decided. Observers, watching for changes after the board finally terminated the CEO have been disappointed. Chair of the US Senate Banking Committee sent a letter to the current CEO in May 2022, that included *"...Wells Fargo's continued inability to manage the basic requirements of serving its customers means that consumers, investors, and employees continue to pay the price. It is clear that Wells Fargo still has a long way to go to fix its governance and risk management before it should be allowed to grow in size. It is unacceptable that after years of failed attempts, nothing seems to have improved."*

The behaviour that resulted in achieving sales goals by essentially creating fraudulent transactions indicated a deep culture problem. Clearly some years later there is still some degree of the problem remaining. To date total fines and penalties amount to over $4 billion. Wells Fargo is an illustration of the challenge of changing culture in a large organization. Attitudes and thinking need to change, led by clear leadership action. The most recent illegal action charges and settlements were in 2021.

4.5   Breach of trust

In what has been described as *"the most widespread miscarriage of justice in UK history"* 72 convictions of former postmasters were overturned by the High Court.

A new system, called Horizon was introduced in the UK Post Office, starting in 1999. From Day 1 employees complained that the system was working incorrectly often reporting cash shortfalls. Leadership of the Post Office disbelieved the employees and required them to make up the shortages from their own pocket. Over 70 branch managers were accused of fraud and false accounting and given criminal convictions. Many went to jail, lost their homes and some died. For twenty years there was a campaign to overturn these erroneous convictions based on the system being flawed.

In late 2019 the Post Office agreed to settle with 555 claimants. It accepted that *"it got things wrong in its dealings with a number of postmasters."* (Got things wrong? I would have thought stronger words were needed!). A number of convictions have been overturned, and court hearings and compensation continue.

A solid example of a toxic culture where management clearly believes consultants ahead of its own employees. This is an organization with a long history of employee – employer relationship issues. This sort of socially irresponsible management only makes efforts to build improved relationships more difficult. Indeed, the culture appears to be the opposite of human centric. Hearing people? Trust?

4.6   Fast paced car company – shocking?

Tesla and its' founder Elon Musk have done am amazing job of revolutionizing the automotive industry. But what is the reality of the culture? After all, the company has built its workforce to almost 100,000 people by the end of 2021. It is said that *"the TESLA culture encourages its workforce to relentlessly come up with new ideas and solutions that meet global market demands."* This culture is founded on Elon Musk's personality and beliefs. TESLA's core values are *"doing your best, taking risk, respect, constant learning and environmental consciousness."*

Yet in spite of this, Fortune magazine reported in June 2022 that the company is fighting a law suit from California Department of Fair Employment and Housing over racial discrimination and harassment. Also, there are complaints from female employees about sexual harassment. A complaint was filed in Federal (US) court by a TESLA investor who accused Musk and the company of *"allowing a toxic workplace culture to fester at the company."* The complaint further alleges that *"TESLA's toxic workplace culture has caused financial harm and irreparable damage to the company's reputation."* Time will tell if the allegations are proven. Innocent until proven guilty.

The culture questions might include - is the stated 'value' of respect just PR? Do actions support the words? Are these isolated cases? Is this a hiring problem – are some of the people being hired not suited to the desired culture? Does TESLA have the wrong people on the bus? There are enough questions that watching the evolution of the company and its human track record will be important as a "responsible business."

It has been said that culture is like concrete. While it can be moulded during construction it later becomes rock hard.

4.7   Big Dog

BrewDog had a meteoric rise from its founding in Scotland in 2007. The brewing company won awards, created a massive band of devoted followers and in many ways, changed the industry. It has been controversial from day one but that was its' goal – to create change in the brewing industry and build a craft beer line superior to anything existing.

Its founders were controversial. They ran afoul of the Portman Group responsible for self-regulation of the brewing industry. In 2009 veteran beer commentator, Roger Protz labelled the owners "lunatic self-publicists" and "over inflated ego maniacs." The company also fell out with animal rights groups early in its existence.

What was going on internally? What was the culture like? In many ways it reflected the values and ethics of the owners. The run-in's with regulators were put down to their desire to change the business. But in 2021 the company and James Watt were hit by allegations from a group called Punks with Purpose and by a BBC documentary that revealed a litany of issues, resulting in 300 employees signing a letter to the CEO about *"presiding over a toxic culture of fear."* There were also allegations of sexual misconduct. The company is also alleged to have broken US federal laws – but no charges have been laid.

Since that time James Watt has apologized and accepted that people were pushed too hard. The company has doubled down on efforts to address cultural problems. Their website currently states *"Whether it be our employees, our customers or the environment, at BrewDog we want to do the right thing!"* Time will tell if their definition of right thing reflects the expectations of others.

4.8   Resource rich

Resource companies have been in the news related to scandals and problems. Canada, said to be home to almost 50% of global mining companies is facing increased scrutiny on the behaviour of these firms internationally. In a report prepared by the Justice and Corporate Accountability Project it stated, *"28 Canadian Mining companies and their subsidiaries were linked to 44 deaths, 403 injuries and 709 cases of criminalization, including arrests, detentions and charges in Latin America between 2000 and 2015."*

The Anglo-Australian company Rio Tinto commissioned its own culture assessment in March 2021 to "better understand, prevent and respond to harmful behaviours in the workplace." The report, released early 2022 cited *"disturbing findings of bullying, sexual harassment, racism and other forms of discrimination throughout the company."* The CEO offered a heartfelt apology and a commitment that findings would be addressed. *"This is not the kind of company we want to be"* he said. Why didn't the CEO know? Was it a low priority? Were managers allowing it to happen because that was the culture – the way we do things around here (because we have always behaved this way)? What was happening when people complained – why were they not being heard?

It is a good sign of being serious about seeking change, to commission and make public such a report – a report that revealed what the real culture is in the business. Rio Tinto should be commended for taking that step. Clearly the culture is not being managed. Mining companies are at the forefront of the cultural challenge. They operate globally, often in undeveloped areas with many indigenous populations. Behaviour is "mission critical." But clearly not managed with equal focus to the task of mining.

4.9   Regulating the regulators

(Press release) Washington D.C., June 28, 2022
The Securities and Exchange Commission today charged Ernst & Young LLP (EY) for cheating by its audit professionals on exams required to obtain and maintain Certified Public Accountant (CPA) licenses, and for withholding evidence of this misconduct from the SEC's Enforcement Division during the Division's investigation of the matter. EY admits the facts underlying the SEC's charges and agrees to pay a $100 million penalty and undertake extensive remedial measures to fix the firm's ethical issues.

CPA's and the firms that they belong to, are a cornerstone in the independent and objective reporting to investors and others on the compliance and health (going concern) of publicly traded companies. They are also, as a self-regulating profession bound by a code of ethics. The ethics codes of all globally recognized accounting bodies have to meet a minimum standard defined by the International Federation of Accountants (IFAC).

Is it a sign of a toxic culture when those charged with reporting on the compliance of business, are themselves operating outside the law? In the UK the FCA (Financial Conduct Authority) has also come under fire for not adequately addressing problems in the financial services industry. As many remember the accountants for ENRON collapsed in 2002, when they were found guilty of obstruction of justice, and "not fulfilling their professional responsibilities."

Managing culture is an even more critical issue, where the public is relaying on organizations that are supposed to be protecting them and ensuring that the "checks and balances" within the system are working.

4.10 Don't mess with rice bowls

The one thing that companies should never do is to make mistakes and problems with employee pay. Not addressing pay problems can lead to a rapid escalation in culture issues and result in a toxic culture. Several high profile examples exist of people related issues that go back to a pay problem.

A report on payroll and employee "leave" issues at Amazon illustrates the challenge. *"The extent of the problem puts in stark relief how Amazon's workers routinely took a back seat to customers during the company's meteoric rise to retail dominance."* In the case of Amazon there is possibly a clear link between a unionization push and a lack of being heard.

The Canadian Federal Government introduced a new pay system called Phoenix. A 2022 CBC headline says it all. *"Phoenix 'nightmare' still haunting public servants, more than 6 years on."*

Another example of problems with people's pay, comes from the UK retailer NEXT. A Sunday Times report in mid 2022, suggested that NEXT had been receiving more than 100 calls a day from employees asking about pay issues, although this has now dropped to around 50 a day. An article in Retail Gazette stated, *"Many of the retailer's workforce have been underpaid over several months following the botched implementation of a new Oracle payroll system that was introduced in February."* It goes on to talk about the major personal issues that resulted – affecting the heath of employees.

These are all examples of how problems with underlying "people processes" can impact efforts to build a positive / non-toxic culture.

4.11 Flying high

No discussion on toxic culture would be complete without reference to Boeing. This company was the very essence of an effective culture – based on safety. Sadly, it seemed to go wrong when the perfect storm hit, and the impact was catastrophic. Not only did people die, but the company reputation was damaged.

An expensive merger was followed by a strategic focus on financial performance. When employees complained that this was causing "corners to be cut" the comments went unheeded. In parallel, the US regulatory agency, the FAA had shifted to allowing more industry self-regulation. In what initially appeared to be a good decision to compete with Airbus, Boeing decided to upgrade the design on their most successful 737 rather than develop a new aircraft, but this brought technical challenges. The company also moved its corporate headquarters away from its traditional operational base to Chicago. As the inquiry into the 737 crashes took place, problems with the assembly of the 787 Dreamliner were also revealed.

The US Justice department, in its' press release of its' settlement with the company stated, *"misleading statements, half-truths, and omissions communicated by Boeing employees to the FAA impeded the government's ability to ensure the safety of the flying public."* One might argue that Boeing lost its balance, and events led to a toxic culture. In a recent statement of the Culture 500 (an interactive index created at MIT[xiv]) it was stated that *Boeing "does not appear to walk the talk when it comes to these (its) stated values."*

4.12 Conclusion

Organizations are complex – like a piece of machinery where every part has to function on an integrated basis for the machine to work. Yet organizations are much harder to effectively integrate than pieces of equipment, because of the human elements.

Efforts to create effective working cultures can be derailed by problems in the operational area. People processes such as pay systems and other support areas are as critical as effective leadership. An organization that "cares" about people will demonstrate this by making sure that the processes that impact people are working effectively.

Leadership sets the example by demonstrating and upholding the values that underlie expected behaviours. The processes demonstrate the reality of this commitment. In the book "Corporate Culture" we discuss why it is imperative to ensure alignment between all policies and procedures and the organizations stated values. (We also provide a tool for how to do it). It is equally critical that "people facing systems" support and enhance the "employee experience."

Leaders should consider at least three core areas that if not working effectively and supporting people, can lead to a toxic culture:

- Poor leadership skills (lack of listening, empathy etc.)
- Poor HR systems (pay rates, pay systems, supports and benefits).
- Poor people facing operational systems (computer based systems as well as processes requiring collaboration to get the job done).

If any one of these is operating at a sub-optimum level it will lead to people issues. Many will be hidden under the surface – but if not understood and addressed, can lead to a toxic culture developing. People will start to believe that "management doesn't care." If public statements are made like "people are our most important asset" – yet day to day issues remain, it eats away at trust and leads to scepticism. If unaddressed (no one is listening or nothing is ever done about it), eventually the gradually decreasing productivity will lead to a toxic culture. Now the problem will have escalated to where there is a culture issue, together with a perception of mistrust, questionable integrity and even a belief that management is lying to employees.

These case examples help illustrate why even the smallest action can start to contribute to a deterioration in culture. No audits will reveal it. No opinion on whether the company is a "going concern" will help investors know of impending issues. Because a toxic culture carries such a high negative impact on any organization, senior leadership must have "their ears to the ground." There must be an early warning system of impending issues. Otherwise traditional actions to enhance performance may bring the desired short term results but will destroy the very system itself.

Corporate Culture

5 How healthy is your culture?

Many organizations may have trouble accepting that they have an issue until it "blows up in their face." Others may believe that they could be doing better, but that their current situation is "no worse than anywhere else." After all, people will always complain about something. Then of course, there are the management "deniers" that believe that people are naturally lazy, and need "aggressive leadership" – a good "kick in the pants" otherwise the job would not get done. Focus on the task.

Several years ago, a management consultant, Paul Stern[xv], who was later to become CEO of Nortel Networks (a company that eventually went into liquidation), suggested in a management book that "the best way to motivate people is to keep them in fear of losing their jobs." This rather "arrogant" leadership thinking is often at the heart of an organization with a toxic culture. The first barrier to get past in determining whether there is a culture issue, is at the most senior levels. There are several barriers or blockers, to discovering whether a culture is good or bad.

5.1 Blockers
Blocker 1
"The emperor has no clothes" syndrome. Individuals, groups, and organizations often develop a view of themselves that blocks them from reality. Some call it being delusional. An individuals' ego would be in this category and stop someone from any sort of personal reflection that might reveal a gap between what they think and what others see. If you can't reflect on your actual individual behaviour, it is going to be tough to see

there is a problem. This topic was the foundation of a leadership book released in 2012 titled "Reflective Leaders and High-Performance organizations." Without an ability to "be reflective" on both self and organizational activity, a leader is not being open to the potential opportunities and needs for change.

Reflection: are you really open to feedback that might suggest what you think about an issue is not, in fact reality as experienced by others?

Organizations also have this problem. This often occurs in successful organizations. If they have become a leader in the marketplace or when they have done such as good job in sharing the corporate "vision" exercise that people no longer check reality. (Vision without reality is hallucination). Often, when people have been around, working for a large organization for a long period of time, they can be referred to as "having drunk the Kool-Aid" (a reference to the historic event at Jonestown, where an evangelic leader convinced his followers that society was out to get them, and there was no hope of survival anyway – so they should drink their Kool-Aid which was laced with poison. It was actually Flavor-Aid).

Reflection: does your organization solicit regular feedback from a broad base of people that have different types of interaction with your business.

Reflection: are you actually, actively hearing feedback in a non-biased open way or just listening and discounting what you believe to be the truth? Hearing everything through your own filter.

Blocker 2

The second challenge is based on the danger of making assumptions. Maybe we could call this the Wizard of Oz syndrome. This problem occurs at the individual level, when people gradually "lose touch" with reality, because of their progression in life. There are many examples of this.

Individuals who have grown up in families that own private companies often feel that they understand the people that work for them – but this is often illusory. While it may have been true when their father or grandfather started the company and worked one-on-one with "regular employees" this might have been true. In fact, the original owner themselves probably came from an average background and grew up with "average people." But as family success grew, the children of the founder might have been sent to private school.

They may have different friends – who come from more privileged backgrounds. The people they meet with socially may have changed. They may "think" they retain an understanding of the average person but that is not the world they grow up in. Often by the third generation, there remains an illusion that the owners are close to the people, but it is often that. An illusion. What is often worse, is that because they exercise the "levers of power," disagreement and dissention - the food of growth, innovation, and creativity is often squashed. People who are perceived as questioning "the way the family does things" are often sidelined.

This can also happen to a degree as an individuals career progresses. In the early stages of careers many people work at the same level but over time, those promoted tend to move out of the ranks of their initial friends and work associated and become more connected to others similar to them in the progression of their careers. The challenge is that this progression often moves managers and leaders away from the people actually doing the work. Reality, that was the food of daily conversations, is gradually replaced by structured input and increasingly analytics. Filtered truth.

The world is evolving fast enough that if a manager has been away from "the front lines" for more than five years, they are probably out of touch about the issues, problems, and challenges that those actually doing the work face on a day to day basis. If management decisions are being made based on a managers belief that they understand the work, because they used to be there doing it, they are probably making increasingly risky decisions.

This also gets worse when a person believes that their success to date has come from the way that they have made decisions in the past. There are often cases where managers who built their careers in traditional "command and control" work environments, fail when they bring these approaches to high technology – or any knowledge based businesses.

How does this link to the wizard of Oz? By assuming that if the desired outcomes are being achieved then the processes and activities being employed to create them are working. More dangerous still is the belief that because "the system" is working, things shouldn't be questioned. This can result in a leaders belief that it is they who are indispensable to the organization. This is the ultimate disconnect between perception and reality.

Reflection: does your life position and experience place you at risk of thinking you understand others, when in fact you are disconnected from their reality? Are you really still in touch with reality?

Reflection: do you honestly believe that organizational success comes mainly from your leadership and the role of others is purely following instructions?

Blocker 3

You. What me? Really? Yes you – as individuals every one of us has the potential to block an honest assessment of a positive or negative culture. It may be because of our personal history – such as in blocker two, but it can also be from our own upbringing and social background. This is increasingly true in a connected world that is multi-national.

In some cultures, individuals are taught to "respect and never question those in authority." In some cultures, there is a clear line between those who have money and typically are the investors, owners, and managers of organizations, and those who don't have money and will always be employees. In these cases, the latter are taught that those with money make the decisions and not to question them.

Another challenge is individual personality. Some people — typically the extroverts, don't wait to be asked their opinions — they deliver them anyway. But introverts tend to wait to be asked and often keep quiet. If one combines this personality of employees with a more extroverted boss who naturally expects people to voice their opinion, what the boss is hearing may be biased and not represent the average employees.

Reflection: as a leader do you actively solicit opinions from the quiet ones' or expect that people will speak up.

Reflection: as a leader, if people are not speaking up do you (incorrectly) assume that everything is OK (no news is good news as the saying goes)?

Reflection: as an individual, are you failing to raise issues and concerns because you don't think it is your place to do so?

Blocker 4

People tend to give up trying to make changes happen, if every time they have done it in the past they have been criticized, scorned, laughed at, ignored – or worse had someone else take credit for their suggestions. This reflects that every organization has a culture – but in some cases it just evolved while in others it has been managed. A culture that has evolved will have developed a whole variety of accepted practices, because "that's the way we do things around here." Not because anyone has actually planned or decided, but because that has evolved into accepted practice.

You always get what you always got if you always do what you always did.

As will be discussed later, culture cannot be left to evolve – it must be understood, defined, developed, embedded, and constantly reinforced. Culture is a strategic underpinning of operational excellence in the knowledge economy.

Knowing that there will be several potential "blockers" to assessing what the current culture level is, one of the best approaches is to engage the employees (and others) in developing a series of questions that need to be asked. What is important is that this needs to be an iterative process with a high level of "front line" involvement. The following chart illustrates the process needed.

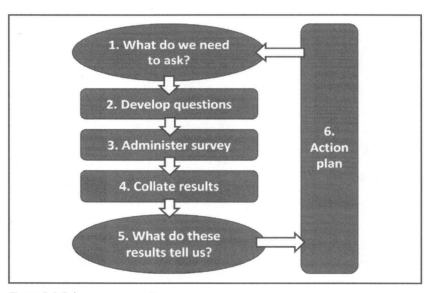

Figure 5-1 Culture assessment

Steps 1 and 5 must be driven by employee input. The main suggestion is using focus groups of some type. The problem with many assessment tools is that they fail to ask the necessary questions. Management or consultants create the list of questions to be asked which often avoids "the hard questions" that may be at the core of an organizations cultural reality.

Some organizations, seeking to take a fresh approach to understanding and addressing its' culture, may put in place a group or team driven initiative. While this must be actively supported by management, the group charged with doing the work must be allowed to act independently. This demonstrates that management wants to know what the reality of the situation is and is ready to hear whatever the results reveal.

A series of questions will be the output from step one. Many consultants already have a series of questions that they might encourage organizations to use. While this may be a good starting point, the questions developed by the group or team must be seen as "getting at the tough stuff" by the employees. Culture is "organization specific" so the questions must reflect this. In chapter two, some examples were given of the attributes of a toxic culture. A great start would be to ask employees to rank "to what degree" these issues are evident in their own organization.

Once a question set has been developed and agreed, the next three steps can be completed – develop, administer, and collate. Again, once these steps are completed and the results summarized, the group or team responsible must take these results back to a series of focus groups, to discuss what the people think that the results mean – and what action might be necessary to fix the problem.

Traditional approaches to employee surveys often end with a report being sent to management. When this happens, management often makes its' own interpretation of what is needed, which may not be what is at the root of the underlying issues. This will result in actions that may be seen as inappropriate by the employees, reducing the credibility of the exercise.

There is also a history of employees believing that any sort of survey or assessment is a waste of time. This links back to blocker number four – the history of the organization. Having employees set and administer the survey will go some way to re-building credibility and offering the same people an opportunity to develop conclusions and recommend action plans will further re-build a belief that "this time it might be different." This group could either be a "culture change group" that is at the centre of efforts to understand and improve the culture, or an ad hoc group created just for this purpose.

In larger organizations the sheer size in undertaking this approach is a problem. One solution might be starting at a divisional or regional level and then gradually "rolling up" the responses. Another challenge is the possibility of intimidation of the group responsible, in terms of reporting back to senior management. Again, one solution maybe either using an independent (external) facilitator that works with the group, and then interfaces with management. The other might be the adoption of the initiative by a member of the "C" suite that has credibility within the organization on a broader basis. This person can then act as the "champion" in working between the group and management. Obviously the best solution is when the group that does the work, can present, and discuss with senior management.

While this approach should be used in the initial "reality check" and development stages it should not form the main basis of a "health assessment" required to sustain a high-performance culture. Constant feedback is required for that purpose, and there are many on-line, real time systems available for this purpose. These ongoing assessments are the equivalent of taking the pulse of the organizations workforce.

There will be constant shifts in attitudes and cultures reflecting the changing activity and reality of the organization – however the key issue is to ensure that the trend is positive, and a high level of "engagement" and commitment is being reflected and sustained.

One very important point is that once an organization develops its' underlying values that drive both behaviour and decision making, these must form the foundation of any feedback system. Questions developed for ongoing assessment including tools like performance assessments for those in leadership positions must use question sets based on the organizations OWN values.

As an example, many organizations use a 360° feedback assessment tool to help guide leadership development. To do this they often use generic question sets – which fail to provide feedback on the very behaviours that the organization has defined as expectations. Thus, the assessment of "reality" is not aligned with stated expectations and any performance problems will not be properly revealed.

The hard questions
Reflective leaders are those who constantly carry out "reality checks" to ensure what they think is happening in their organization is in fact the reality that people are experiencing. This quality is essential when being open enough to hearing about and accepting potential issues that may reveal either an existing toxic workplace culture or provide insight into a developing risk of one being created by default. How about asking questions like these?

Do your PR messages (externally) resonate with employees as credible and accurate?

Do you consider the role of front line supervisors as the most important?

Do you allow front line supervisors flexibility in addressing employee issues?

Is senior management hearing the truth about internal relationships?

Are you receiving honest answers from people who leave? (Do you check independent 3rd party sites like Glassdoor on a regular basis?)

Are supervisors at all levels rewarded for upholding the organizations' values?

Is culture actively talked about and promoted?

When was the last time that an independent culture assessment was carried out (NOT a survey – but one on one's).

How is the culture integrated into the strategic business plan?

How is culture being measured and tracked?

What are the behavioural drivers of our culture and how do we know these are being perpetuated on a daily basis?

Are regular discussions taking place about better aligning actual decisions and behaviour against plans and expectations?

Does our behaviour reflect the expectations of employees, customers, suppliers, and others? How do we know?

Are employees ever embarrassed by decisions the company makes?

Experience from working with organizations shows that when asked to rank the importance of task focus and relationship focus, most organizations give themselves a higher score on task.

5.2 Blind spots

A second challenge in assessing reality, comes from personalities. As individuals we all possess a certain combination of personality attributes. None of us is "perfect" – we all have certain areas that are stronger than others. These attributes are also evident in leadership styles – so wherever a person is in an organization, these personality attributes might impact their ability to see and hear others.

"Knowing self" is important as a life skill. It is said the better we know ourselves, the more able we are to understand other people. We have some general awareness – even if we have not individually investigated our own personality. But our personal awareness is sometimes flawed – we have blind spots.

Different leaders will use their natural skills in different ways; research has shown that while certain skills are important for leaders – such as communications, each individual will tend to "lead" from their natural strengths.

While it is beyond this book to delve into this specialized area more fully, the major leadership styles appear to be of four general approaches. Visionary (Inspirational), Relationship (People), Task focused (Drive), and Process (Data / Detail).

Examples of blind spots can be created by either a lack of a certain attribute or by the assumption that others share that attribute. As an example.

Visionary leaders understand "big picture" thinking and may not realize others don't share this. They also may also not realize that being a visionary thinker, they worry less about detail, yet process oriented leaders and (individuals) may consider this highly important. Visionary leaders can be great but can frustrate those who are more task or day-to-day detail oriented. Those who believe that any decision must be made on solid facts and evidence might be increasingly frustrated by visionary managers who only require a certain level of data before they make a decision.

The strength of an organization is the ability to collaboratively blend these different "views of the world" into a cohesive "whole." If the whole team were detail oriented, slow decision making would result. If no data was used, then risky decisions would be made. Again, the different people bring "the balance" required.

Business tends to be natural task oriented, so one way of assessing the ability to "think" about relationships is to ask the question.

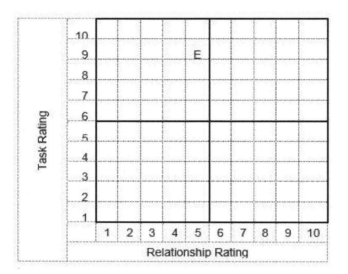

This matrix is a simple scale of one to ten on thinking about task and about relationships. A quick way is to rate yourself on each scale, and then rate where you think the people around you are on the scale. This can be your team members on a leadership team or your workgroup.

There is no right or wrong answer – but in seeking to address culture – which is all about relationships in a world that is more traditionally task oriented, this sheet and the ratings shown can be a valuable **conversation piece** to start assessing awareness of relationships among associated in the workplace.

6 Culture and the workforce

In a knowledge economy, THE key resource is people – or human capital as it is referred to. People not only bring the knowledge, skills, and experience that an organization needs to function, they also generate collective value, through their combined ability to work together. This is a classic case of the value created by a workforce being greater than the "sum of the parts." This is part of intangible infrastructure.

The value that is created by having an engaged, motivated, and productive workforce is composed of three key attributes – and it is the <u>combination</u> of these three that create competitive advantage and enhance organizational value and performance. These three components are:

- The individuals in the workforce.
- The collective workforce, and
- Workforce compatibility.

When people are hired they fill pre-determined positions. The organization seeks out the desired skills, qualifications and experience and offers individuals positions based on market rates of compensation. This forms the basis of the cost of the workforce. But while managing cost is important, management's real focus in building an effective business model, is in creating a system that integrates all the components, including people, in a way that maximizes value creation. So, the cost of a workforce and the value of a workforce are two entirely different aspects.

This is a critical distinction. Cost is an input, and traditionally organizations have sought to minimize input costs per unit of output. Payroll and compensation costs are tightly controlled as they form a major part of an organization's operating expenses. However, while cost is important, the ability to create and nurture a workforce that achieves maximum value is the key issue.

> **You can have the most qualified and highly talented workforce in the world, but it is their ability to work together that creates organizational value.**

This is why culture is so important. Culture is the crucible within which resources are brought together (by management within their business model) to create the desired outputs and outcomes at the highest level of sustainable productivity possible. Cutting input costs might increase value per unit of output but enhancing the operation of the crucible will likely have a much greater, leveraged return.

Costs are driven by who is hired. Value is created by how well management integrates and leverages the skills and capabilities – the potential, of those who have been hired.

6.1   The individuals in the workforce

The individual workforce deals with the hiring and compensation of individuals that are needed for the collective workforce. This is the value creation potential provided by the individuals.

Focusing on hiring and retaining a talented workforce is a key role in assembling the resources required for any business model. A talented workforce provides the potential for value creation. A toxic culture will lead to three issues at the individual level.

1. A poor reputation will negatively impact hiring.
2. Poor experience once hired will lead to higher turnover.
3. The individual potential will be limited due to poor motivation.

In order to be competitive and maximize value creation, the culture needs to be seen as a strategic component that allows the organization to attract and retain the talented workforce required.

Organizations also face the need to train and develop individuals within the workforce. These costs of individual development should be seen as investments in the workforce, intended to leverage people's individual ability to create value.

6.2   Collective human capital

Collective human capital deals with the effectiveness of people to people, human relationships once hired. This is the value creation potential for the combined workforce interacting with each other.

Accelerating or leveraging human capital comes from the ability of the organization to encourage collaboration, cooperation, and communication between people. The value of human capital comes from building the collective capacity of the people assembled who make up the workforce. Areas such as developing team skills, collaboration and cooperation, silo busting, group problem solving, plus all areas of supervisory and management skills. All these investments are made to build the capability of the collective workforce. As the word "collective" suggests, expenditures on communicating strategy, linking it to the persons job and all activities related to morale building and motivation are essential aspects of leveraging human capital.

Many of these attributes come from the collaborative ability of the workforce, which is often driven, not by individual education, skills, and experience but by emotional responses to the work environment. The type of workplace created determines the level of individual commitment and engagement with value creating activity. A growing focus is on behaviours in the workplace and helping people and "teams" understand how they can work more effectively together by understanding the interaction of different individuals. A toxic culture has the potential stop this collective building of a value creation model. People will "do their jobs" and follow instructions, but they will not feel encouraged to take the risk of sharing ideas or working closely with others. Thus, a toxic culture will cause problems in "the collective:":

1. Minimizing of personal risk taking.
2. Job protection and silo building.
3. Poor communication and sharing of information.
4. Added bureaucracy (people will not take their own initiative).

This mobilization of collective talent becomes even more important when relationship building forms a critical part of an organization's business model. Today, an organizations workforce is no longer made up of only employees. There may still be fulltime employees, but these are supplemented by temporary, seasonal, and part time and contract individuals. All of these will require effective working relationships – in addition to the traditional internal relationships.

There will also be relationships with external organizations on both the supply side – the supply chain, and on the sales and distribution channels. The more effectively these different elements of the workforce collaborate, communicate, and cooperate, the greater will be the value creation capability of the total business model. A poor or toxic culture will lead to:

1. Greater disputes between partners.
2. The "blame game" when problems occur.
3. Slow operational action (opposite of lean and agile).
4. Unwillingness to share information and opportunity.

Eliminating these problems with the collective effectiveness of the total workforce are critical in ensuring the optimum operation and value creation of an organization's business model. (Leaders also need to realize that major financial investments are made in putting many of these collaborative arrangements in place, and such investment is lost or depleted when human behaviour fails to leverage the approach and associated investment).

A final aspect of this segment of collective human capital is the effectiveness of those tasked with "enabling" people to work together. This task falls both to individuals themselves but mainly to people in leadership positions. This can be group, team, section, business, or any other position that has the responsibility of managing, coaching, supporting, and enabling people to work together. Poor leadership shows up in a toxic culture by allowing:

1. Passive and active discrimination, harassment, and bullying.
2. Disrespectful, abuse, poor inclusiveness, unfairness.
3. Arguments, intolerance, disputes, lying, unethical behaviour.
4. Misunderstanding, unreasonable goals and objectives.

While some of these issues will be discussed in the next sub section related to "structure" (i.e., the policies and procedures), the reality is that no matter what structural systems are put in place, leadership behaviour will demonstrate whether an organization REALLY believes in certain values as part of its' culture – or is just paying lip-service.

6.3   Enabling compatibility

This is the ability of the organization to create value or to leverage the combination of human capital within the overall business system. Much of this depends on the effectiveness of the operational work environment.

Each business exists for a purpose and its business model is created to be "fit for purpose." The model takes the necessary inputs and brings these together or integrates them through processes, projects, activities, and tasks to create outputs. The combined outputs enable the organization to achieve the desired outcomes from the model. A toxic culture might exhibit the following barriers to value creation:

1. Wasted time – the necessary tools and support are not available.
2. Frustration – human / equipment interface operates poorly.
3. Stress – trying to work with inadequate systems.
4. Health problems – physical / mental health.
5. Overload – systems don't work to support desired performance.
6. Mistrust – inability of management to fix systems.

The more effectively management designs, builds, and operates this overall model the greater the value of the business. This is where the term "enabling compatibility" comes in. Compatibility between different resources within the business model determine its' effective functioning. For example, when using machines, the human / machine interface must be optimized for maximum effectiveness; in the mining sector, the machine / natural capital interface must be compatible.

In a capital-intensive business, equipment manufacturers made the necessary investments as part of the equipment cost to maximize operator compatibility. In good software design, systems are created with optimum human interfaces to maximize effective interaction.

The more effectively the business model creates its "compatibility interactions" the greater the performance. When "capitals" are brought together to convert inputs to outputs, the processes through which this happens are designed for optimum performance. In the past a great deal of attention has been focused on task, activity, and process improvement but if this is not fully integrated and engineered into human performance factors, the result will be negative.

This is the area of culture development that many organizations overlook – preferring to focus on pay, benefits and other direct aspects for the individual. Great organizations with great cultures tend to ensure that their business model is developed with people at the core. Human compensation is, after all one of the greatest costs. Why not ensure that nothing gets in the way of ensuring that every aspects of a persons work is "enabled" to the highest degree possible? That every aspect that involves human capital has been evaluated for maximum / optimum compatibility.

Another reason this aspect is often overlooked is that it involves peoples emotional response within the workplace. Frustration, boredom, wasted time, and stress are all driven by a work environment that a person is subjected to.

As will be discussed later, this issue of alignment and integration between all business model resources being utilized is an important aspect of creating a positive culture.

Corporate Culture

7 Human performance filter

One of the best ways to think about the impact that a poor or toxic culture has, is to think about the work environment being like a filter through which peoples talents have to pass to bring benefit to each other and the whole organization.

Figure 7-1 The cultural filter that impacts value creation

The cleaner the filter, the greater the utilization of human potential and the greater the value created. The workplace refers to "the cultural battlefield" because for many, that is what it is.

Many people become frustrated with work, because they bring their potential – all their willingness, interest, qualifications, and motivation, but often feel that they have to fight to be able to do a good job. If management is not aware of issues, challenges and problems that get in the way of people doing a good job – eventually the people will lose heart. They may stay and just do the work they are paid to do – but their potential to add value, individually and collectively will be severely depleted.

The workplace represents the reality of the business model that management creates to convert strategy into action. It reflects the bringing together of all the necessary resources including people. Is it possible that the "great resignation" following COVID is a reflection on the challenges posed by a dysfunctional business models? The solution will not be paying people more money because the problem has to do with, more often than not an emotional response to the workplace.

7.1   Some battlefield experiences

What are some of the typical examples of business model issues that are incompatible with building an effective workplace? Using the topics on the filter, we can look at specific aspects within any typical business model. Readers can think about their own experiences.

Bureaucracy

There are typically several drivers of bureaucracy in a business. First is the willingness of people to work together for a common goal. Where there is not a clearly shared "purpose" or where people don't understand how they fit into the organization's goals and objectives. Conflicting objectives between departments. Managers who want to avoid any risk by making a decision that follows procedures. When no procedure is in place, then the decision is escalated.

Very often organizations talk about being agile and responsive, and wanting people to innovate and take risk – yet the approval and decision making process seems to be designed for the opposite effect. One of the most challenging areas is the need to balance internal controls for minimizing operational risk taking, with a freedom for action necessary to motivate people to act. Concerns over privacy, data security, cross functional access to information – all can contribute to bureaucracy that gets in the way of getting the job done and slows things down. While essential control requirements must be met, the people productivity aspects must be an important consideration.

Bureaucracy starts at the top in the way the organization is structured but is also impacted by how people in leadership positions behave. If leadership is hierarchical and focuses on command and control, the result will be bureaucracy. What employees see in their day-to-day work will define the level of bureaucracy – not what management talks about.

Matrix organizations are often created to "allow" cross functional collaboration, but it matters little what type of organization chart exists. What matters is whether people are encouraged and are willing to freely collaborate.

Poor systems
It is often strange that highly qualified technical staff are often asked to work on outdated systems. Computers and technology generally are an enabler to human talent. Efforts to save money by cutting back on investment necessary to keep technology up to date, will cause poor productivity and frustration – yet in many organizations this never actually show up anywhere in management reporting. It is part of the hidden composite impact of overall system performance, but it has a major role to play in employee value creation. All that management knows is that "cost input to output is too high."

There can be many system frustrations, and these may overlap with bureaucracy. Approval systems to buy items needed for work. Technical support systems and response times. Passwords and back-up protocols.

Blame
A healthy culture seeks to learn by its mistakes, but a poor or toxic culture focuses on blame, searches for the guilty and hides issues. Many people have no problem in admitting to mistakes and do not need a manager, supervisor or even work associate "calling them out" on it. Eventually no one wants to try anything new or risk having something go wrong. The culture becomes one of fear of reprisals rather than encouraging innovation.

Lack of trust
Trust is a core foundation of many of the other problems that occur. Where trust exists, information, help, and support will flow freely. In a knowledge economy, information is a core commodity that must move quickly and freely between people engaged in achieving the goals of the organization. If individuals trust each other then barriers to sharing will fall.

Many organizations have made significant investments in knowledge management systems (KMS). Collecting, indexing, and making available "knowledge" that can be used and freely shared across an organization. Yet many have sub-optimized the benefits because people are either unwilling to input their knowledge into the system or spend the time accessing it. In some cases, a focus on things like "billable hours" in service organizations can actually penalize those who try and use the KMS.

Trust is something earned - not freely provided. Re-building trust from poor past experiences will take time. People may start by distrusting management and will need to be convinced of the integrity and authenticity of people in management positions. If people hear management saying one thing but doing another, trust will be damaged. Frequent movement of supervisors across roles may be good for the supervisors work experience but may be damaging to building an effective culture. It is all about balance.

Unfairness

This problem can be both structural – in the way procedures are developed for how people are selected, hired, promoted, or compensated. It can also be selective and behavioural, particularly at the supervisory level. People in positions of authority can by-pass established procedures and act in a way that others see as unfair. An example might be how the opportunities for overtime or extra shifts are allocated or offered.

Different treatment for people at different levels in an organization can be a source of festering frustration around unfairness. This might be in procedures such as time off or travel policies or other benefits offered to staff.

Some may say the solution is the serenity prayer that says "..grant me the serenity to accept the things I cannot change, courage to change the things I can, and wisdom to know the difference." This is all well and good but pre-supposes that human beings are rational people that can evaluate a situation and come to a logical conclusion – upon which they will base their actions.

But while people can indeed be logical, their "feelings," that are a key driver of behaviour often intervene. Intellectually people will know that there are some things they cannot get fixed but knowing this and accepting it in a way that has zero impact on their performance might be a "bridge too far!" In a later chapter we will return to this issue of how emotions impact motivation and the "quality of the culture" and will also discuss the impact that unique personalities have on responses.

Miscommunication

One of the foundational aspects of a high performance culture is clear communications. People who tend to be worried about how others might mis-interpret their words sometimes resort to saying nothing at all. Others will not ask for explanations for the fear of being made to look foolish or stupid. Creating an environment where there is no fear, and a high degree of trust is a pre-requisite for clear communications. Clear communications are also a pre-requisite for collaboration and cooperation – essential for innovation and creativity.

Part of communication that is often forgotten – is listening. Even when a culture "allows" people to speak out, there may be poor communications because the listeners either "discount" the sources of information or are pre-disposed to make judgements. A toxic culture that demonstrates exclusion, and discrimination, and allows rumours, gossip, bullying and other negative behaviours will not allow effective communications. Additionally, the situation is often made worse by "unspoken" communication such as attitudes and body language.

Poor resources
Workload is a key driver of a toxic work culture. An environment where there appears to be no appreciation by those planning and scheduling work, of their impact on others. This typically reflects a bias towards task, driven by managers and supervisors that may score high on management skills but low on leadership skills.

While historically the terms "manager and leader" have been used interchangeably, it is clear that the underlying skills are significantly different. Managers tend to focus on task while leaders tend to focus on relationships. Relationships "enable" the effective and productive execution of task. It, like many issues around managing resources, is all about balance.

Figure 7-2 looks at the balance between management / task and leadership / relationships. A high task / low relationship focus (Q1) will tend to be "win / lose." It reflects the hierarchical organization structure, where results are driven by exercising power over people. Intimidation and fear tend to be predominant.

Q2 is the "powerless" zone - lose / lose because neither task nor relationships are being "managed" effectively. Q3 is dangerous as it reflects low task high relationship; there is the potential for results but until task is improved it is "powerless."

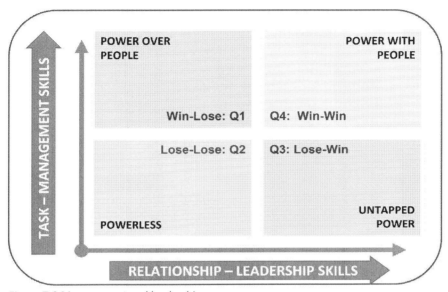

Figure 7-2 Management and leadership

While Q1 and Q2 can both be the foundation for a toxic culture, Q3 can also be a problem. Eventually people will get tired of all the "people stuff" and will want to put their talents to use. People usually want to be stimulated and challenged by their work and an environment that fails to do that can be just as bad as one where there is zero attention to people relationships.

A balance, driven be enhanced leadership skills, achieves task by exercising power with people. The quadrant marked Q4 is considered win / win. There is a good working environment, but the job gets done effectively. The link with effective use of resources, tends to come from a belief that management needs to "push people to get results" and assumes motivation is extrinsic not intrinsic.

The reality is that motivation can be stimulated by extrinsic factors but is ultimately a decision by the individual – made as much by logic as by emotional response. Leaders create a working environment where people WANT to perform. Creating an environment of fear – whether it be fear for ones' job or fear of retribution, or fear over being made to look bad – will all contribute to de-motivation and the creation of a toxic culture.

Leaders who don't "see how others see them" are often unaware of how their behaviour may in fact be creating unwanted results. Some may have a personality that intimidates other people. They may not actually "be" intimidating – let alone see themselves as such. But if that is the impression that they give, that is what people will see as reality. Once again, the importance of understanding human behaviour – especially for those in leadership positions is critical.

As a matter of interest, some people are not just intimidated by the personality of their leaders, but they are also intimidated by the "title" and "authority" that a leader has. Senior managers often make the mistake that they come across as approachable – yet many employees would never dare to raise issues with them.

Silos
While hierarchical organization structures (such as those behind Q1) tend to build silos, it is the working of relationships that determine the reality of whether these functional silos help or hinder performance. If the leaders in the organization tend to collaborate and cooperate well, this will tend to permeate down through the organization and move the actual working relationships towards Q4. If this type of behaviour is encouraged, the reality of the organization chart will be a secondary issue.

Leaders may tend to pay lip service to cooperation and collaboration – but the reality of the workplace and the culture will reflect what people see happening. Using the picture in Figure 7-3 managers will keep their "silo drawbridge that protect their castle" raised to stop intruders until they are convinced it is safe to do so.

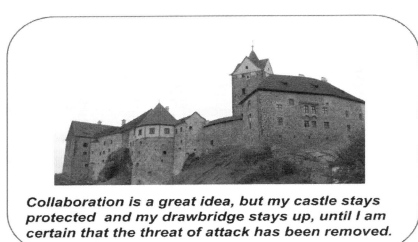

Collaboration is a great idea, but my castle stays protected and my drawbridge stays up, until I am certain that the threat of attack has been removed.

Figure 7-3 Silos and protection

If there is an absence of trust, and people knowingly withhold information, then the reality will be a culture of protectionism.

Discrimination

Many organizations believe that if they implement policies and procedures, supported by "awareness training," to guard against discrimination, then problems will be eliminated. These organizations report on their hiring practices and demonstrate their broad base of minorities in the workforce as proof of lack of discrimination. Additionally, they will run training and development programmes that make managers and staff aware of discrimination and how to avoid it.

Reality may reflect a different picture. If attitudes, values, and beliefs are not actually changing, there will be passive discrimination evident in the way people treat each other. These attitudes, unless "called out" and dealt with by others in the workforce, especially supervisors, will spread and undermine efforts to build barriers to any type of discrimination. Such behaviour is often referred to as "passive aggressive."

If supervisors exhibit these behaviours it becomes even more difficult as people may be reluctant to "challenge authority." This is another case where the selection, development, and evaluation of people in leadership positions becomes such an important aspect of building a positive culture.

Personal agendas

Every person working in an organization should be focused on actions necessary to achieve the collective agenda.

> **An organization is a collection of people brought together to achieve a common and shared purpose.**

Culture is a reflection on how well this simple expression of purpose is actually working. Sadly, in many situations people act in a way that is driven by personal agendas. The desire to "get ahead' by putting down others – in the belief that "looking good" with management will bring rewards and promotion. The desire to deflect blame onto others to avoid have to admit having made a mistake – including fear of reprisals. Managers sometimes sub-consciously reinforce this by treating some people in a more positive way than others.

Personal agendas cannot be entirely eliminated, but leaders should be aware of behaviours that may negatively impact the desired culture and act to clearly demonstrate that this type of approach is unfair and self-serving and is to be avoided. (This is why "getting to know your people" is such a critical aspect of anyone in a leadership role).

Argument

"Every time I raise an issue I seem to get into an argument in trying to defend my position." Not an unusual comment from people who are faced with an unwillingness to listen when they a bearers of bad news or come forward with ideas. This is not to say that questioning and debate are bad. One organization has a phrase in its corporate values that encouraged "constructive dissonance." They actually want debate - they want people to question things. But they also want people in leadership positions to be open to the opinions of others. Plus they want those raising to problems to have thought about ideas for solutions.

Very often arguments become a way of life when unfairness is present. Having to argue against forced overtime or schedules that don't respect personal obligations or commitments. Requests for deviations to "corporate policy" where a special situation has occurred. Every time these happen, they can chip away at the culture. Not to say that argument will never happen – clearly there will be some unavoidable disagreements – but great supervisors, managers and other leaders will be able to listen to the requests in a reasonable manner and avoid reacting.

To be fair to supervisors and managers – who are also often under time pressures and may find it simpler just to cut off any debate, this measured response and avoiding reaction is often hard. But that is the essence of effective leadership. This can be a growing area of discontent; it seems that the ability to have a reasoned discussion with others when views differ, is often met with aggression and rudeness.

Intolerance

If we describe someone as intolerant, this usually means that they do not accept behavior and opinions that are different from their own. This sort of closed thinking creates a toxic culture as it stops any debate of ideas, thoughts, and opinions on any subject. People using this approach often want either to sustain the status quo or to return to some "perfect" way of doing things, based on their own opinions alone. Intolerance also shows up as a passive response to discrimination – deciding whether someone is "worthy of listening to" based on their race, colour, creed, or any other quality that differs.

This behaviour is often demonstrated by people who are referred to as narcissists.

Gustavo Razzetti[xvi], the CEO of consulting firm Fearless Culture, in an article written in 2020, makes this statement. *"The problem with narcissists is that they want to be admired and feel superior – rather than leading others, they want to dominate them. Multiple studies show that, although most people think narcissists are effective leaders, the reality shows that they are not. They will abuse power to get what they want, not what the company needs – rather than building culture, they destroy from within."*

While this links back to the importance of the selection process used to recruit and appoint people to leadership positions, it is not limited to leaders. People elsewhere in a workforce may also have these tendencies. In a culture that requires people to collaborate and cooperate this behaviour on an individual basis is a problem.

This behaviour not only stops dead any cooperation, it also destroys organizational commitments in areas like diversity and inclusion. While people may be sent on training courses and "buy in" to approaches of tolerance, engagement, and inclusion, deep down they don't believe in it – and their day-to-day actions will reflect his.

Inconsistency
Some may look at this issue and argue that in a rapidly changing business world, inconsistency is the reality we live with. Agreed – but in one-on-one relationships people become more open if trust has developed, and one of the prime creators of suspicion and lack of trust is inconsistency of behaviour.

"I just don't know we you are coming from?"

Poor management communication is a prime driver of this challenge at the middle management level. These managers and supervisors are often seen acting inconsistently by their staff and team members, but often this is caused by lack of communication and direction from senior management. Middle managers feel like the "meat in the sandwich." Expected to keep their employees positive and motivated, yet being forced to deliver inconsistent policies, direction, and information.

Senior managers are the one's that communicate high level intent and direction. Mid level managers and supervisors are in the position of either communicating this information downward or converting the senior managers "intent" into action, so that day-to-day work can be accomplished.

If the message that mid-level managers and supervisors are hearing keeps changing, their own credibility suffers. Sometimes senior managers are unaware of how their own behaviour may be causing issues "lower down." This is where reflective leadership, and the tough question about exactly how much information to share become important.

A good example comes from a company that was working on its culture and had set seven strategic priorities. These were revenue growth, product quality, sales, employees, productivity, cost, and schedule. This was causing some confusion, so it was decided to ask the leadership, middle managers and supervisors and employees what they thought the company priorities were, based on what they observed in day-to-day work.

Some might conclude that there could be no right answer – that they are all important. The problem is that while correct, the reality is that front line managers and their staff have to make judgement decisions on a daily basis between conflicting priorities. If they are to do this successfully they need to know that their priorities are consistent with management expectations.

Each set of responses show the average of the team ratings. Each person responding rated the seven items from most important to least important. Thus, if all respondents rating something as the top priority, it would score seven.

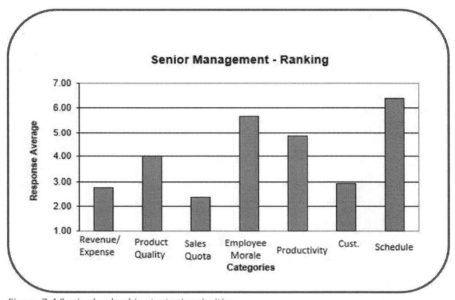

Figure 7-4 Senior leadership strategic priorities

The first series of responses shown, were obtained from the senior leadership team – the one's setting strategy and priorities, and responsible for communicating these to the rest of the organization. So, it appears that almost every senior manager ranked "schedule" as the top priority – i.e., an average score of about 6.3.

Senior management also indicated that employees and employee morale was almost as important as schedule (people are our greatest asset); an importance ranking of almost six out of seven. It is difficult to rank strategic priorities, but these responses were based on what message senior leadership felt was being delivered within the organization. "Here's how we do things around here."

Next were the rankings from the front line employees – the largest group of respondents. This is what they believed were the priorities.

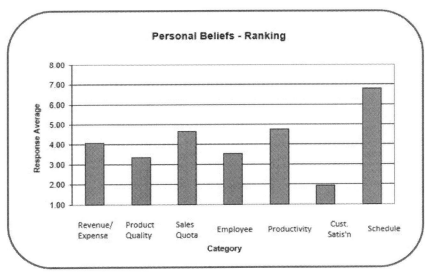

Figure 7-5 Employee beliefs based on observation

What the leadership thought were the rankings, were not the message that employees were receiving based on day-to-day observations and priorities. In fact, they saw schedule, revenue, sales quota, and productivity all more important than employees and employee morale.

Sadly, customer satisfaction ranked at the bottom of the list. (Although senior management had also ranked it low which was a surprise!). One can see the "task" aspect coming through clearly in that "schedule" is consistently at the top of the list and both productivity and sales quota would be closely associated with task / activity.

There is no right solution here – but what should exist is some level of connection between senior management and employees. This was a mid sized company so some level of communication challenge would have existed – but these results clearly showed a difference on how important employees saw themselves in the order of things. How about mid-management.

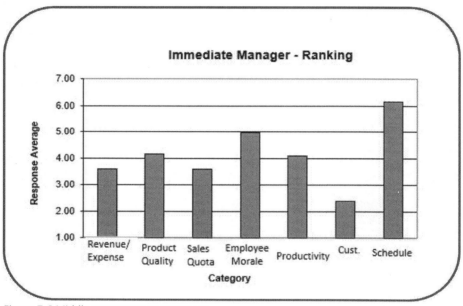

Figure 7-6 Middle management responses

The middle management results tended toward a flattening out – trying to reflect both the priorities of senior leadership – their bosses, while at the same time trying to deliver the message of being "employee / people oriented." These managers clearly see the importance of delivering results and focusing on task.

Inconsistency of strategic priorities is critical – but so are many other messages. Fairness. Inclusiveness, Customer focus. Agility. Performance. Delivering a consistent message when everything is important is a challenge. This is why organizations that focus on culture, start with people first or people-centric approaches. The belief is, supported by surveys such as those from Gallup "if you look after your people, all else will follow." The famous phrase "culture eats strategy for breakfast" by Peter Drucker is also worth remembering.

Favouritism

Finally, the underpinning of unfairness. Exhibiting favouritism is a normal human response. There are certain people we like more. Certain people we believe are "more like us." Certain people that always seem to be willing to "go the extra mile" and are there when help is needed. The challenge is that when anyone acts this way it creates a negative impact on the culture. While some just "shrug it off" others, rightly so feel that it is exhibiting a behaviour that creates exclusion and segregation.

This is an important issue for anyone in a leadership position. Within any team there will be people who are more amenable to positive responses in certain situations, and it is tempting to take this approach to avoid argument and work with someone who thinks the same as "we do."

7.2   Cleaning the filter

There are several approaches that are needed, and which must be part of "managing the culture" if these problems are to be avoided. Remember – the cleaner the filter the more engaged and productive people will be. The greater the leverage from human capital. The pillars of building an effective culture are:

1. Start at the top – making people centric approaches a foundation of corporate strategy and built into governance framework.
2. Establish and promote expectations of acceptable behaviour (these are often called "corporate values").
3. Ensure a hiring and orientation approach that supports the desired behaviours and beliefs.

4. Focus continually on leadership selection, performance feedback and development.
5. Ensure operational policies, procedures, processes, and tasks are structured to align and support people's needs.
6. Establish and sustain approaches that encourage and support input and feedback for improvement.

How to implement all of these steps are the subject of another book[1]. There are also many credible consulting organizations that can help identify an organizations requirements to build an effective culture – but exercise caution. YOUR culture is unique to your organization and must embrace its business reality, its history, its ownership, and other unique foundations. Avoid trying to copy others – focus on developing what is right for your own organization.

For the CEO or board looking for the "silver bullet" for cultural shift – I'm sorry – there isn't one. In fact, if that's how you believe you can solve the challenge of eliminating a toxic culture or managing to sustain a positive one, you have already made your first, big mistake.

In the chapter on the case studies, review both the Boeing and Wells Fargo – possible the BrewDog events. Only time will tell if the past events that demonstrated a toxic culture have in fact been resolved. If the result is positive that will be very commendable for leadership. (Return to look at the real time result of the Culture 500 – this will provide updated assessment of some of these challenges).

---

[1] Corporate Culture: Combining Purpose and Values

8 People and Profit

Many organizations have been successful, focusing on generating a good return on their investment (ROI) for their shareholders, and seeing the human dimension as a cost to be minimized. These organizations have worried little about culture. "Remember, I sign your paycheck" we hear. "Appreciate the fact that you have a job – your lucky to be here." For many, people / employees, were seen as a commodity based resource. Hire people when you need them and lay them off when demand falls. People in many situations required little training and were "interchangeable."

The battle rages on around focusing on the cost of "human resources." One opinion sees the money paid to people as an investment but for many it is a "sunk cost." It goes straight to the cost of sales. Pay people less and profits will increase the theory goes. For many, the ultimate measure of success of a "for profit" corporation is that it maximizes profits for its shareholders. It is relatively easy to connect the cost of payroll to profits and demonstrate the relationship. Cut payroll costs and profits rise. However, for years studies have been conducted that maximizing profits by focusing on the <u>cost</u> of people alone, while bringing short term results, often has longer lasting negative effects.

Management gurus have historically focused on issues around managing the work force for maximum productivity. Effective work scheduling. Process improvements. Capital investments. Broad based information and knowledge sharing using computer based systems. The human resources department has focused on the role that training and development has on performance and productivity. Employee performance assessment systems have been put in place to evaluate peoples work. Pay for performance systems have been developed to link cost to output. Incentive programs have been developed to encourage motivated employees to higher levels of performance. Job descriptions, competency frameworks, pay equity programs. Benefit programs that form part of an organizations offerings to employees to attract and retain talent.

In the "age of manufacturing" the profession of industrial engineering became an essential component of planning and managing work activity, including the "man / machine" interface. Time standards were established for tasks to be completed. Daily, weekly, and monthly reports compared the "allowed time" to the actual time, and reasons for variances were thoroughly investigated.

The importance of working on the "non task" or relationship aspects of managing people was also not left out. Foundational theories of motivation were initially developed in the 1950's and put in place with three specific theories. Maslow – The Hierarchy of Needs Theory. Theory X and Theory Y by McGregor and the two-factor theory of Herzberg[xvii]. These formed the basis of management training for motivation in the 1960's and 1970's – when many "baby boom" individuals were climbing the management ladder. Little surprise that some of these beliefs remain in organizations.

Work continued in developing theories and practise around motivation, but the concept of organizational culture is only now starting to gain prominence. There have been two major drivers for culture to become a critical strategic initiative,

8.1 The first driver – culture underpins competitiveness
The first real focus on culture came from the drive for competitiveness in global manufacturing in the 1970's and 1980's, especially when the Japanese started to make major inroads into the automotive market, as

well as electronics. Those who studied Japanese management methods quickly realized that while there was a heavy focus on effective process management, this was matched with an equally strong focus on the culture. Books like "The Toyota Way" began to explain how this balancing of task management with human management and leadership, appeared to be the foundation of competitive advantage.

While many who were seeking improvement, readily adapted Japanese ideas like Hoshin Kanri planning, Kaizen, JIT (Just in Time) delivery, 5S, Poka-Yoke, SMED and other task focused areas, they often failed to realize the intended benefits. Massive investments were made in developing 6 Sigma approaches to process improvement, to lean manufacturing and to statistical process control (SPC). For many short term benefits were delivered in terms of "bottom line" improvements. But many also had trouble sustaining these efforts and initiatives and making them part of the way things were done on a routine basis. Many implementations were undertaken as improvement projects, with the help and support of armies of management consultants.

International standards were also developed to try and provide organizations with simple, standardized frameworks that could be implemented in any organization seeking to sustain improvement initiatives. One of the most famous, the ISO 9000 series was started in 1987 There are over a million organizations now certified to ISO 9000, however the approach has garnered criticism and almost a third of annual renewals (the certificate lasts for three years) choose not to maintain their certification – for any number of reasons. Clearly there was limited ROI and the approach "didn't stick." Approaches often fail to stick because they do not become part of the culture – they are just another project, another layer of work and complexity added to an already over-burdened workforce.

During this time, the era of organizational excellence awards became a high priority for many organizations to demonstrate their leadership in performance. Programs such as the Baldrige award in the USA, the EFQM in Europe and the NQI Awards for Excellence in Canada – together with many other national, state, and other recognition awards were available. One important aspect of these awards was that they focused on an organization <u>as an integrated system</u>. The concept of a business model came into vogue that identified the key areas of the business model involved in creating a framework for excellence in performance.

Central to these was process (task) management – but they also brought in other key aspects that needed to be integrated and to function and interact effectively. This included people and the concept of leadership.

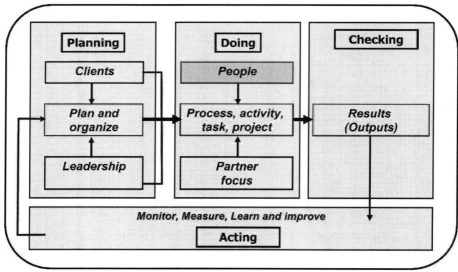

Figure 8-1 The foundational business model

The business model was the framework that management built, capable of achieving the desired outcomes. It involved bringing together resources and creating a system of integrating these resources to convert inputs to outputs. This "thinking" of a business model was to become instrumental in the growing importance of culture. Culture is the human relationships that exist when all of the components of the model are brought together.

While there had been a heavy focus on task improvement, achieving a true cultural change where these task / process focused initiatives become embedded effectively as a way of life leading to competitive advantage was been less successful. This was because the tasks shifted from being focus on human / equipment inter-dependencies to human to human relationships. This brings us to the second major driver that was occurring at this time.

Business models are not new – these are what business managers create that reflect the unique requirements for their own business. This is why culture must also be seen as "business unique." It is important also to note that the concept of the business "model" in central to the current ideas of integrated thinking and reporting.

8.2   The second driver - culture and the service economy

This second driver of change was the shift in the way work was done – both in the type of tasks performed as well as the growth in non-manufacturing organizations. While many of the approaches to process improvement were equally applicable to non-manufacturing work processes (although many organizations chose not to expand their improvement efforts in these areas), the major shift was the "jobs" became more specialized and required skilled and semi-skilled staff more than unskilled positions.

While in manufacturing the majority of work involved in converting inputs to outputs required people to interact with machines, less people were required as more machinery was automated. However, employment in the technical skills areas grew as more people were required to support this automation – both in creating, supporting, and developing the equipment but in seeking ways to make it more productive within a particular work environment. As the service economy and now the knowledge economy developed, the effectiveness with which people interacted with other people became increasingly important.

Thus, the focus on culture brings a) an understanding human interactions with other humans and b) a recognition that these human interactions permeate every aspect of the business model.

The more effectively people interact with one another, the greater leverage that an organization creates within its business model. While process and task are important and still form the basis of converting inputs to outputs, the level of human engagement, commitment, and motivation determine to what degree the capabilities of these systems are leveraged to create value. As can be seen from the business model, (figure 7-1), the scale and scope of culture expands well past employees to all other interactions within the system. These include:

- Employee to employee (the workforce of all types – full time, part time, temporary, contract).
- Individual to supervisor (all levels, between and among anyone in the organization).
- Organizational workforce to suppliers and other external partners (effectiveness of the supply chain).
- Organizational workforce to clients, customers and the "output chain."
- Organizational workforce to other "partners" – financiers, regulators, local government, society generally.
- Organizational workforce to the task, activities, processes, and projects that are used to convert inputs to outputs.
- Organizational workforce to the other aspects of the business framework they work within (policies, procedures).

Employee engagement is often seen as the same as culture, but this is incorrect. Employee engagement is a sub-set of culture – an outcome measure of having an effective / positive culture. A toxic culture will never allow employee engagement to fully develop. Culture is about optimizing all relationships that people have, with everything that impacts their ability to perform.

A toxic culture is one where the business model or business system is hampered by poor relationships. People cannot perform to their level of ability and eventually the organization develops a reputation for having a negative culture.

The organization may still be operating – may even be generating a profit. But the human potential and capability is not being used as a competitive advantage. Additionally, the organization may be seen as increasingly out of touch with other key components of their business model. Which brings us to the impact of a business on the wider society within which it operates.

Corporate Culture

9 Culture and responsible business

Recent years have seen an increasing call for greater accountability and responsibility from business as a member of society. It has also been suggested that shifting an organizations focus from shareholders to stakeholders might help this improvement. The Business Roundtable, a group of US CEO's, has issued a commitment that focusing on corporate purpose will help this transition. Maybe. Maybe not.

Firstly, business needs to make a profit and satisfy its shareholders. The whole foundation of capitalism requires this. To try and minimize this requirement would be unrealistic. However, most investors – real investors and shareholders anyway, want their investment to be reasonably safe and secure. They want the business model, that currently generates income to remain in operation, healthy and profitable.

The whole responsible business movement faces challenges. Many boards and CEO's probably already feel that they ARE a responsible business. So, what is the problem? The issue is that a certain level of discomfort has grown about business behaviour – which is the behaviour from the actins and activities of the organization – therefore behaviours driven by the people in the organization – especially leadership. If in doubt refer back to the case studies in chapter four.

Criticism of business conduct has been heightened by the press which is quick to pick up on negative aspects. Whenever there is a scandal of any type, it is widely reported and often adds fire to the calls for action and change. The challenge business faces is that there are some things that it can truly manage and control and some things that society may frown upon and criticize, but which a business is faced with addressing. For the discussion of toxic cultures, these need to be split into three streams of concern.

1. Problems related to illegal activity by the business – by design or by mistake.
2. Problems that come from the way the business is run – that are clearly and directly related to culture and behaviour.
3. Problems that come from the competitive market place that any organization has to respond to in order to address competitive advantage and a level playing field.

9.1   Illegal activity

First, business is a "member of society" – with the same rights and privileges of an individual. As an encyclopedia defines the legal position of a corporation *"A corporation has separate legal personality in the sense that it is a legal person separate and distinct from its shareholders, directors, and officers. A corporation may enter into contracts and own property in the same manner as a natural person. The corporation may also sue and be sued in its own name. A corporation may also be convicted of a criminal offence provided that the criminal provision provides for a fine in lieu of imprisonment."*

Society has created a legal framework for corporate governance, so that corporations can be formed as collectives to carry out activities as part of the economic fabric. Corporations must abide by the law, many of which are the same as individual laws but many which apply just to corporations – often also relevant to their status e.g., publicly listed versus private corporations. Many scandals are driven by behaviour that involved breaking the law, usually for one of three reasons:

- By honest accident or mistake.

- By actions that have been agreed to and condoned by leadership.
- Actions taken by individuals on their own.

All three of these come from the way the business is run. While it is often not clear what the exact reason is, the result can be expensive. In the last twenty years according to the website Violation Tracker, there have been almost half a million legal fines, penalties and awards related to illegal corporate actions. These fines amounted to almost half a TRILLION dollars. Poor culture that results in illegal actions is expensive. Many of these fines were for reporting, disclosure and regulatory problems; but these fines and penalties include areas such as employment standards, health and safety and others where inadequate consideration of people working in the business was present.

Irresponsible leadership plays a key role in this first stream of problems. It is either not clear that the organization has an expectation of abiding by the law, or it is considered that breaking the law is part of doing business in a competitive market and if you are "found out" the fines and penalties are just part of the cost of doing business. This has a significant negative impact on many people internally as well as external stakeholders, and contributes to a toxic culture.

Most people in society find this socially unacceptable. When leaders, both directors and senior executives are seen to "get away" with this, there are calls for business to "clean up its act." For the board to take hold and provide better oversight. Where this is "part of the culture" then it is a clear example of a socially toxic and socially unacceptable approach to business.

9.2   Poor leadership

In the second stream of concerns, poor leadership is again the cause. Although actions may not result in legal non-compliance – such as labour laws and health and safety, the behaviour and relationships between people are not operating as within a reasonable society. This is referred to as "socially acceptable behaviour." Social norms are the unwritten rules of beliefs, attitudes, and behaviors that are considered acceptable in a particular social group or culture. Norms provide us with an expected idea of how to behave, and function to provide order and predictability in society. Given that organizations are expected to reflect the society within which they operate, then they would reflect those social norms.

The challenge is that actual behaviour may drift away from the "norms" that are expected. It is the job of leaders to reinforce acceptable expectations of behaviour. In business this requires at least a minimum discussion and agreement because organizations are often "supra societal" – employing and working with different people from different backgrounds where "norms" may not be the same.

The sort of behaviour that society would consider abnormal would include. bullying, victimization, sexual or any other type of harassment, discrimination, abuse – physical or verbal and others. A great example of unacceptable behaviours is given in the HR guidelines of Cambridge University. These include:

- Aggressive or abusive behaviour, such as shouting or personal insults.
- Spreading malicious rumours or gossip or insulting someone.
- Discrimination or harassment.
- Unwanted physical contact.
- Stalking.
- Offensive comments/jokes or body language.
- Publishing, circulating, or displaying pornographic, racist, sexually suggestive, or otherwise offensive material or pictures.
- Isolation, deliberate exclusion and/or non co-operation at work.
- Persistent and unreasonable criticism.

- Unreasonable demands and impossible targets.
- Coercion, such as pressure to subscribe to a particular political or religious belief.

Some years ago, a movie was released called "The Corporation" that explored organizational behaviour. It was suggested that corporations had started to behave like "clinically diagnosed psychopaths." This was that they acted as *"..social predators who charm, manipulate, and ruthlessly plow their way through life, leaving a broad trail of broken hearts, shattered expectations, and empty wallets. Completely lacking in conscience and in feelings for others, they selfishly take what they want and do as they please, violating social norms and expectations without the slightest sense of guilt or regret[2]."*

This might be considered extreme, but it has contributed to the body of opinion that modern corporations exhibit socially unacceptable behaviour. Where corporate thinking is that "if there is no law telling me that I can't do something, then obviously I can" the problem is compounded. (This is a core issue around thinking that corporations should be "principle based" not just rules based). Certain areas of "unacceptable social behaviour" will gradually work their way into legal requirements. Examples are diversity, equity, and inclusion. An effectively functional adoption of DE&I is a core attribute of an effective culture.

9.3 Business and "generally accepted" unethical behaviour

Finally, the third area of concern. This is often the more problematic. This is the issue of ethical behaviour. As corporations are subject to law, if they do something that is legal but ethically unacceptable or considered socially deviant, they cannot be legally prosecuted for it. In a competitive local, national, and global environment the laws are different between national boundaries. Thus, what might be legal in one country is illegal in another.

---

[2] Hare, R. D. (1993). Without conscience: "The disturbing world of the psychopaths among us". New York, NY: Guilford Press.

This is where multi-national organizations legally engage in "gaming the system."

No where does this have a greater impact on corporate reputation than in the field of tax planning. Even if the leadership of a company accepts that it is unethical to practise tax avoidance (not tax evasion as this would be illegal) it is highly unlikely to actually change practice and increase its own taxes payable as this would place it at a competitive disadvantage. The investors would complain. The board would complain. In fact, is some jurisdictions it would be illegal for management or the board to take this action and therefore deplete investors equity (earnings and value).

So even if organizations profess to be "ethical in everything they do" it is going to be almost impossible to reconcile this with the legal framework within which they operate. This has two results. First the people involved with the organization – its workforce and others will look at this and say "hey – that's unethical. Obviously you say one thing and do another." Credibility and efforts to build a culture that often includes "acting ethically" will be negatively impacted.

The second impact will be the "field day" that the press and others will have with this. Stories about corporate (and individual) tax avoidance make great headlines. This impacts corporate brand, reputation, and credibility yet there is little that can be legally done. The problem is large. Recent estimates suggest that tax avoidance is costing countries economies nearly $500 billion per year. This has a major impact on the societies that organizations operate within. National finances are impacted leading to social problems, issues, and challenges. Inadequate funding for education, highways, health care, social benefits, and many others impacting possibly some of the employees directly but having a far greater impact on the people of the society that is being "short changed" on taxes.

Where does this leave organizations, striving to improve their image and operate as "valued members of society?" Those seeking to be a responsible business? Primarily organizations must do everything in their power to be seen to act and behave as responsible (including ethical) members of society. This means creating a culture focused on developing and sustaining the most positive relationships possible with all key stakeholders.

Organizations need to do a better job of addressing the conflict between the publics perception and desire for ethical behaviour and the reality that business faces in working within the "rules of the game." This may involve better global tax collaboration (which has started but seems doomed) as well as business doing a far better job of communicating the impacts of areas like tax planning on their global operations.

Some businesses do clearly care about their communities. There are many examples of charitable donations and support for educational programs and other initiatives to address racism, diversity, and other important causes. Many organizations support initiatives such as Habitat for Humanity and the United Way.

The passion that drives these causes must expand to addressing issues such as minimizing the usage of scarce resources – such as saving water and eliminating pollution. In reality many issues related to the organization and its' impact on the "heath and sustainability of society" come back to caring. The ultimate question a responsible business needs to ask itself is "are we operating in an ethical manner that reflects the values of the society we live in?" Limiting behaviour to that required by law, clearly brings business into conflict with being a responsible member of society.

9.4   Building a responsible business

An effective corporate culture will establish the foundations for the goal of being a responsible business. Setting out clear expectations and reporting against these issues and challenges to the society within which they operate, will help re-build corporate reputations. Many groups and organizations have been developing to help these efforts. These include

- Responsible Business 2030.
- International Institute for Sustainable Development
- Frank Bold.
- Just Capital.
- B Corp.
- And many others.

There are also major changes occurring in corporate governance requirements and corporate performance and compliance reporting. Regulators are becoming more focused on "the whole system" of corporate performance. International entities are encouraging a broader based whole system approach to business management.

One thing is certain. Becoming a responsible business must be based on an effective culture to guide behaviour including all aspects of leadership and management decision making.

This discussion comes full circle to people and profit. While eliminating toxic cultures is critical for future success, losing sight of the importance of sustaining profitable operations is equally critical. It is not either / or but both. The best way to demonstrate the criticality of achieving balance is through a case study / story.

Many people may not have heard of Bill Norris – yet for many he epitomized the coming together of business and social responsibility, especially as it related to the world of technology and "managing a successful growth business and also doing good for society" over and above the economic impacts.

Bill Norris was a pioneer, working in the computer business just after World War II, when he and other US Navy cryptographers formed

Engineering Research Associates (ERA) to build scientific computers. He hired forty of the members of his codebreaking team. In the 1950's when ERA hit a drought in government contracts and funding, it was sold to Remington Rand. Initially ERA operated within Remington Rand as a separate division, but a later merger with Sperry Corporation created Sperry Rand, and the ERA division was merged into a company called UNIVAC. This resulted in most of ERA's work being dropped. Many employees left and set up a new company named Control Data (CDC), unanimously selecting Norris as president.

This team went on to develop the early super-computers. In a legal battle with IBM, who at the time was working to develop its' own advanced machines, Norris and Control Data won over $600 million in legal settlement. He went on the expand the business in a broad range of computer areas. However, his strategic thinking was impacted in 1967 when Norris attended a seminar for CEO's, where Whitney Young, who at the time was head of the National Urban League, spoke about the social and economic injustices in the lives of young black Americans.

This speech, along with a summer of violence in Norris's hometown of Minneapolis, greatly disturbed him. He became a champion of moving factories into the inner cities, providing stable incomes and "high-tech" training to thousands of people who would otherwise have little chance at either. He also invested heavily in computer based education. An online teaching and instruction system developed at the University of Illinois at Urbana–Champaign, called PLATO was at the heart of applying technology to societal problems.

The university developed most of the system on a CDC-computer but driving graphics terminals of their own design. In 1974 they reached an agreement with CDC to sell PLATO in exchange for free machines on which to run it. Computer based education was in its' infancy in the 1970's, but CDC was also engaged in education through its' successful CDI's or Control Data Institutes and professional development institutes. At this time the company was still doing well financially, using its technological leadership for competitive advantage, and offering an attractive place to work.

The company sought to embed their approach and commitment to balancing societal needs and making money, in its corporate values and mission. Every new employee worldwide attended an orientation program where they were presented with the gold coloured engraved plaque on which were listed the company values. The treatment of people ranked high in importance as did the balance of running a commercial business but also doing good.

But the company failed. By the 1970's the company had become a multi-billion, global corporation, engaged in most areas of computer technology. With the creation of the micro-processor in the late 1970's and early 1980's, the whole computer industry was upended. Every division of CDC – mainframe computers, peripherals - such as data storage devices, education, and computer support services, such as engineering and consulting services all needed investment – and there was just not enough cash to go around. In its' desire to apply technology to social needs there were just too many drains on cash. In effect it lost focus of its core business – the cash generation machine that allowed it to invest in newly emerging areas. To create the balance.

The lesson is that you can do all the right "people stuff" and be socially minded, even building whole business areas that are addressing newly emerging societal needs like education. But the foundation must be a healthy core business. You cannot be socially responsible in how you operate if you lose control of your core business. Socially responsible business MUST be a combination of making money for shareholders PLUS operating for the benefit of society. An equal focus on effectiveness in WHAT you do with an underlying culture that defines how you do it.

10 Leading versus managing

Culture is about relationships. A culture that builds and sustains effective relationships between all key stakeholders is imperative for strategic success in the knowledge economy. It is also a foundation upon which efforts to enhance and build responsible businesses will be based. This in turn rests upon enhancing the approaches to the leadership and management of people.

In all honesty and reality this is a challenge. Even in one-on-one relationships such as two people living together this poses challenges. When this is "scaled up" into organizations, especially those employing a large number of people it becomes one of the greatest challenges that management faces.

Traditional approaches to management were easier. Command and control allowed managers to focus on what needed to be done, and then issue instructions and orders to people to go and do it. A managers role was to oversee work execution and be accountable for keeping activities on track and achieving desired outputs. Time devoted to "the needs of people" was limited, and often seen as the role of the HR department. Management told people both what to do and how to do it.

The workforce was often viewed and treated as a homogeneous group, bound by policies and procedures that needed to be followed. When issues with workforce were not handled effectively by management, people in the workforce often sought to bring a union in, as their representatives to negotiate on their behalf with management. While unions continue with this role, their membership has been dropping. Workforces have become more individual, with people having a greater ability provide or withdraw their services without a negative personal impact. Leadership qualities have historically been considered part of the role of management – but as the theories on motivation and increasingly human behaviour have been developed, there has been an increased realizations that leadership skills are profoundly different from management skills.

With organizations already focusing significant time and effort on improving task activity, it was becoming increasingly evident that if people were not involved, engaged, and committed, it mattered little how effective the processes were, the results fell below expectations.

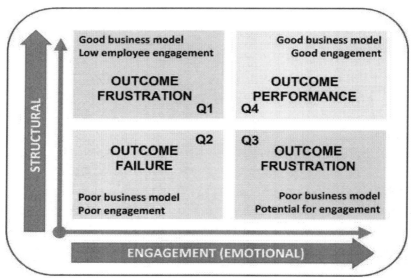

Figure 10-1 Lack of management / leadership balance

Building on the four quadrants discussed earlier, the failure to balance the structural aspects of business and the emotional can be demonstrated, especially on the outcome of the business model.

Figure 9-1 suggests that there are four aspects to balancing structural and engagement / emotional aspects. The outcome goal in Q4 is the achievement or exceeding of desired performance – while Q1 and Q3 create frustration and, if not addressed Q2 ends in business system failure.

The low task (structural), low relationship approach in Q2 creates an outcome which is business failure. Poor people engagement and support and poor processes and structural development of the business model. Eventually in a competitive market these will lead to failure.

Q1 is often where organizations operate – high attention to structure, and all the attributes around task. Relationships that are left to develop on their own. No focus on the culture or "managing" the work environment. The outcome is frustration of management and workforce. This outcome of frustration in Q1 is felt mostly by senior management; major investments have been made in structural changes and improvements – enhancing tools, equipment, processes and even approaches to HR policies and procedures – yet the results still fall short.

Q3 is a sad place to be. The organization is people oriented, trying to do the right things, but the infrastructure within which people work is not operating effectively. The outcome is frustration, and in this case is most felt by the employees. It is a great place to work; relationships are effective, and people get on with one another. But the problems that employees face is that the whole business "infrastructure" that they must work within – systems, policies and procedures, tools, and equipment – are all not "fit or purpose."

Interestingly employee turnover is probably driven by both Q1 and Q3 frustration. Either senior leadership pushes harder and harder on employees to deliver the results without improving the relationships required for collaboration, communication and cooperation, or the employees just get fed up and leave because the system and process – the tools that allow the person to do their job, are not working correctly. This would include things like the payroll systems outline in the earlier case examples. It is also worth remembering that on exit interviews many of these people will place the reason for leaving as "getting a better job." Maybe they mean one where they have the tools and equipment to actually achieve their goals and objectives.

Q4 is where we want to be – a balance of having created a functional business model with the tools, equipment, and other structural aspects necessary to enable the employees performance PLUS the creation of a work environment that not only creates no infrastructure barriers but also produces a "crucible" within which the work required takes place effectively. Management and investors are happy with performance and the workforce is happy to be there.

Efforts to enhance "structural" aspects of the business model (converting inputs to outputs), raise the left hand scale performance, but fail to deliver the desired outputs. Today's focus on organizational culture and employee engagement reflects the growing realization that to enhance and achieve optimum performance, working WITH people is a requirement. The working group that developed the ISO 9001 series of quality management standards – concluded that culture was an integral part of enhancing performance when they released ISO 10010[xviii] in August 2022. The accompanying release note states that *"this document gives guidance on the evaluation, development, and improvement of organizational quality culture to help an organization to achieve sustained success. This document takes into account the fundamental concepts and quality management principles, with specific focus on **people engagement and leadership.***

In many organizations, large investments have been made in enhancing infrastructure – new systems and the application of new technology. Disciplined approaches to the development of processes, activities, tasks, and projects (the methods through which "task" is achieved). Part of the reason for this is that there is usually a clear financial justification in enhancing the execution of task. An ROI can be calculated on a new piece of equipment or a new system – but developing an ROI on investments related to relationship building and much harder to develop.

Organizations can calculate high level outcome measures such as output / employee, but these are amalgamations of total system performance. Developing cause and effect justifications on spending related to enhanced relationships must be developed at a more micro level. Efforts have been made to justify training and development expenditures in this way and while helping, are currently far from a perfect solution.

Current approaches to measures human performance can be quite misleading. One key indicator being used is HC-ROI or human capital return on investment. It is suggested that this measures provides a metric that can demonstrate the effectiveness of HR management in an organization. While there is indeed a correlation between progressive HR practices and an enhanced HC-ROI, there is limited cause and effect relationship.

There are many indicators that demonstrate a strong correlation between employee engagement, culture, and organizational performance. Not only HC-ROI but strong, credible surveys such as the Gallup Q12 Meta analysis. Thus, part of the challenge is that the decisions to adopt an effective culture is somewhat a strategic shift based on faith and belief. This is why senior, board / CEO led strategy on culture development is critical. It is not a program or an initiative – it is a strategic approach to the way business is run.

> **Managers need people to direct and control.**
> **Leaders need followers**

If leaders at any level are not "believers" in this type of approach to managing and leading people, the strategy will fail – or at a minimum be sub-optimized. The workforce will see leaders as being inconsistent, not trustworthy and having little integrity; as a result, engagement will fall well short of plans or possibilities. Morale and productivity will suffer.

Effective leadership must reflect a shift from management skills to leadership skills – from "power over people" to "power with / through people."

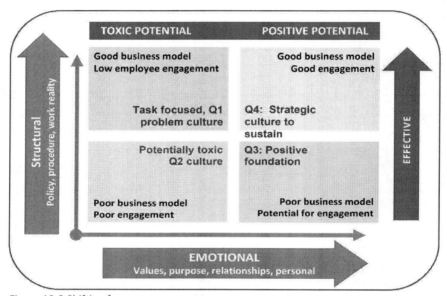

Figure 10-2 Shifting from management to engagement

This is very much an emotionally driven attachment. The people make the decision to be led, so leadership is something earned not something created by position in an organization chart. Figure 9-2 shows the shift required to move from an organization having, or having the risk of a toxic culture, to one where the culture delivers positive outcome potential.

In Q2 we have the "worst of all worlds;" an organization with a poor management model, combined with poor engagement / relationships which is the greatest risk for a toxic culture.

Traditional approaches to improve performance often shift the organization to Q1. The business model – all the "structural stuff" is addressed but "it's management that knows best." Employee involvement and engagement remain low – and even though the organization may be performing because of its' investments in infrastructure, it will be sup-optimizing outputs and will still face the risk of a toxic culture. (Many high growth, high technology organizations face this risk – working on the basis that high earnings potential and a challenging job will make up for poor treatment of people). Eventually it "catches-up such as in Activision Blizzard.

In Q3 we have the "great place to work" challenge. Great attention has been paid to enhancing people factors, but the underlying infrastructure is poor. While people often initially react to this as a positive opportunity (us against the world syndrome), if infrastructure problems are not addressed, they will become de-motivated and demoralized. Performance will drop, and / or key people will leave.

Q3 is also where problems occur when there is a lack of leadership integrity. The infrastructure policies and procedures may be in place – but in practise - the reality of day-to-day operations, this is NOT what people in the workforce see happening. A poor track record on ethics would fall into this category. Supervisors pay lip service to diversity and inclusion. This – to use the environmental term, would be the equivalent of "people green-washing."

Q4 once again is where we want to be. People are provided with the framework to perform and leaders that encourage, respect, and support them. Leaders who "do what they say they do." Leaders who have committed to the desired expectations of behaviour in the organization and lead by example. Managements challenge at Q4 is to ensure they can sustain the desired culture.

In order to make the shift to Q4 there needs to be a solid understanding and acceptance of human behaviour and the emotional aspects that drive it. There are two core aspects that are at the foundation of understanding how to develop "followers." It is beyond this book to go into the level of detail required to fully appreciate the importance and impact of tools and methods now available to support these needs. However, the three core aspects that must be understood and addressed are:

- People have unique personalities that are a combination of capabilities at varying levels of development.
- Different people will react in different ways to similar situations based on both their perceptions and their personality.
- Human responses are complex – combining emotions and logic, driven by personality, experience and underlying values.

The first thing that this tells you is that treating the workforce as a homogeneous "mass" will not work. It is why the one-on-one relationship between a member of the workforce and their immediate supervisor is of prime importance. Readers may want to delve into the important role that immediate supervision plays in organizations such as Toyota (several of the books related to this are listed in the bibliography).

Organizations need to "understand" their workforce to the highest level possible. They also need to develop and communicate values related to behaviour to every member of the workforce so that expectations are clear. Supervisors need to be well trained in, and understand human behaviour, and be selected and promoted on their ability to sustain and develop the workforce as well as deliver results. Frequent feedback systems must ensure that expected behaviour is reflecting and sustaining the values communicated. There must be an open approach to improvement, willing to hear feedback about what is working and what can be improved.

Without going into the use an application of tools and approaches that focus on understanding people and behaviour, there are some core aspects that EVERY organization that is serious about developing leaders and having these people as the core stewards of a positive culture, must include:

- Hire for attitude. Talent is a combinations of skills, education, experience, and knowledge. Attitude is the enabler of using these talents effectively.
- Know what you are hiring. Resumes, bios, and references are not enough. Use a personality assessment tool as part of the hiring process. (Avoid pure "typing" – people are much more than types in pre-defined boxes).
- Use personality tools in the preparation and development of every single person who is being placed in or considered for a supervisory position. They must clearly understand their own personality, how they are seen by others and how others might respond to them. This will help them understand others.
- Use personality assessment tools in ALL group and team development. In every situation of high interaction, understanding people and their behaviour is a key skill.
- Be consistent with what tools you use. There must be a consistent framework for human development approaches and tools so that a shared understanding is based on common language.

Leadership development is much more that providing communication skills or the traditional approaches of planning, managing, and supporting. The outcomes from great leadership development approaches include people who can coach, support and advocate for their staff as well as enable their collective success.

Management skills remain a core component of executing task, but leadership skills are the component that explores how to build followers by understanding productive interactions, based on personality, logic, and emotions. Work is managed by managers, but a toxic culture is either created by or allowed to evolve by poor leadership.

11 Toxic people

Toxic cultures by definition include toxic people – so this book would not be complete without addressing the issue.

While leadership is faced with the challenge of ensuring toxic people are not part of the workforce, there is the question about what to do when it becomes clear that there is a problem person involved? The best solution is avoidance – ensuring that toxic people never become part of the workforce.

11.1 Getting the right people "on the bus"

A workplace is like a journey on a bus. Once the passengers are on the bus they need to figure out how to get along. Hiring people is like stopping at the bus stop to pick up passengers – so avoiding toxic employees must start with ensuring that only the right people are allowed to get on.

Hiring processes must include tools to help determine the type of person the candidate really is. The risk of hiring a potentially toxic employee is critical. Research quoted on a site that provides computer based systems to help the hiring process quotes that *"hiring one toxic employee into a team of 20 people, raised the risk of the other nineteen seeking employment elsewhere by 54%."*

Past behaviour is a good indicator of the potential for future problems. While references are often hard to obtain, efforts should be made to ask questions such as:

Would you re-hire him/her if the opportunity arose?

How well did he / she collaborate and cooperate with others?

Were relationships with other peer employees positive and successful?

If people reported to this individual, how good was the relationship?

If a manager / supervisor, were transfers and resignations higher than elsewhere?

Were there ever situations where this person behaved in a way that discredited your organization?

Using assessment tools and testing should be a core step in evaluating candidates. Many are available – but just "typing" is not adequate to assess potential "toxicity." One approach is available from a company called Lumina Learning[xix] called the "Spark" assessment. This provides visibility into behavioural qualities such as being accommodating, collaborative, empathetic and adaptable. It also looks at sociability, competitive, tough, reliable, practical and many others.

While the actual relative scores on each quality is helpful, this information can provide specific support to questions to be asked in an interview process. The interview allows two things -probing the individuals responses to specific questions as well as observing overall behaviour. Questions should be formulated and agreed before the interview – although unstructured discussion can also be of value. Multiple interviewing is also important to view the candidate through different eyes.

Interview questions should consider that qualities suggested by the assessment and would also include:

What five words or personal qualities would your former manager use to describe you?

What five words would people who worked for you use to describe you?

What three qualities would your peers describe you adding to the workplace?

What are your top three strengths that you bring to the workplace?

What are three areas of personality and skills that you are currently working on developing and improving?

Were there any times when you had to deal with personal conflict at work. What did you do?

Were there times where you felt stressed dealing with other people? What was the problem and how did you resolve it?

Did you ever reflect back on a situation and feel that you could have handled things better? Can you give a few examples?

Have there been any situations where you have dealt with people who were difficult to work with? What was the problem and how did you deal with it?

Describe three situations in which you showed exceptional leadership skills

Carefully listening to the person's responses will provide good insights into their personal behaviour and qualities as well as the maturity of self-awareness. These questions should provide confidence that the individual is aware their own qualities and behaviours and to what degree these impact interaction with others. It is also important to watch for body language. What behaviours should be looked for?

Over-confidence and trying to appear superior / arrogant.

Boasting about their skills and accomplishments.

Talking about "me" versus "we" when presenting achievements – particularly as a manager / leader.

Poor behaviour towards anyone they meet outside the interview – e.g., the receptionist or other staff members.

Approach to respecting time – were they on time? Do they appear "fidgety"

Lack of attention – even things like accessing their phone (did they have their phone turned off to give you their full attention?)

Negative attitude towards past employers and co-workers

Shifting blame for problems, such as poor results and difficult work situations.

Always trying to deflect problems onto others rather than admitting mistakes or taking personal responsibility.

Clear signs of poor attitude – such as discrimination towards others conducting the interview.

Negative generalizations about others – women, immigrants, people of colour and others.

Particularly look out for signs of arrogance and possible narcissism. In our book on corporate culture, the importance of hiring is dealt with in more detail. In terms of the costs of a poor or toxic culture, investing in the interview and hiring process is a "preventative" action. It may add costs to hiring but its' benefit will be seen down the line with less workplace disruption, greater cooperation, and collaboration, and lower turnover.

11.2 Handling the hiring mistakes

A toxic culture is often reinforced by the way a company deals with people that have joined the workplace, but who start to exhibit problems. If not addressed quickly, problems will escalate and start to "poison" the workplace atmosphere. The goal is to avoid this by having an effective hiring process but also by taking action on problems if they occur.

The first point should be obvious. When a problem like this occurs use it is a learning experience asking, "what went wrong and how can we amend our approach / hiring process in the future?" The natural next step might be to fire the individual. But wait – the decision to hire was a mutual decision. The organization offered a job to a person – so what responsibility does the organization have? Some organizations will actually acknowledge the inadequacy of their hiring process and have every employee on a probationary period. Upon reflection this might risk being a one sided solution – although it can be argued it gives the candidate the chance to "look behind the curtain" as in the Wizard of Oz only to find out that the company did a great "selling job" in the interview but reality is not like that once they start work.

The best situation from a poor hire is that both parties agree it was a mutual mistake and agree to part company. However, organizations must be cautious when the decision of a poor fit seems to be one sided. Honest and open conversations are needed to try and discover why the need to "part company" has arisen. Maybe the organization did not make its values and expectations clear during both the interview and orientation? Maybe inadequate training was provided that increased the risk of problems on the job? There are two sources that provide good additional thoughts on this issue of hiring failures and have been identified in the endnotes.[xxxxi]

11.3 Dealing with the seeds of toxic behaviour
One of the challenges with people is that they are complex. Personality has been discussed as has the emotional impact on actions and decision making. One of the most difficult challenges is where previously good, motivated, engaged, and effective people start to behave in a different way.

They may become argumentative. They may react in an unusual way when asked to work with another team or on a project that they would previously have welcomed. They may arrive late or seem to be pre-occupied with something. They may receive distracting message – phone calls, texts, e-mails. They may start taking time off and asking for unusual vacation days. These are likely not turning into problem employees but are experiencing some personal change that is impacting "who they are."

People cannot leave their personal or home life at the door of the workplace. In the way that if something negative happens at work it can affect ones home life, the reverse is true. Organizations cannot take the attitude that what happens outside work is of no concern – equally they must take responsibility for what happens in the work place. This is again where effective supervision comes into play. It is also the type of situation where having an EAP or Employee Assistance Program becomes important.

While a supervisor should constantly monitor employee behaviour, they should be careful in dealing with such changes in behaviour. The risk could be minor or major – possibly leading to violence or even suicide. Generally, a supervisor needs help in responding to the situation, so their first step is probably to have a low key discussion with the employee and then seek advice.

In today's current environment of growing awareness of mental health problems, steps to watch out for are:

Mental health	Work behaviour
Appearance of paranoia, worry, or anxiety.	Concern or worry over assigned work. People are "ganging up" on me
Long-lasting sadness or irritability.	Reactive, argumentative, quick to anger, appear depressed
Extreme changes in moods.	Enthusiastic and then disinterested
Social withdrawal.	Eating lunch alone, not mixing, avoid group activity, not wanting to be on project team
Dramatic changes in eating or sleeping pattern.	Visible weight changes, bleary eyes, lack of job concentration, arrives late

The table above shows five typical behaviour issues that might demonstrate mental health issues and in the next column the way in which these may be revealed in the workplace.

The important issue to address is to avoid any toxic behaviour growing and impacting the workplace. Someone observing possible issues should escalate to someone who can give advice. The steps suggested including:

Observe the individuals actions over a period of time and circumstances.
Analyze the observed behaviours (is there an issue?).
Approach the individual on a low key basis to talk about observations.
Seek advice if required from others and "experts."
Follow up to see that action is being taken.

The drift towards behaviour that may become toxic needs to be stopped early. Either the supervisor and employee can deal with the issue or help from other managers — if it is an inter-departmental issue, or the HR department. Whatever action is taken, the impact must be considered on both the individual and the co-workers. It also must be conducive to sustaining a positive culture — i.e., be seen as fair, timely, honest, and caring.

11.4 Toxic external relationships
While much of the leadership of people is concentrated within a business unit, the reality is that dis-functional and toxic behaviour can also occur with external relationships. Customers, suppliers, regulators, auditors, and many others. To the degree that these impact the effectiveness of a business model they must be dealt with.

Prevention is a primary focus. This is why organizations seeking to build a positive and productive culture and to minimize the risk of toxic behaviour must seek to partner with others who share their values. In the same way that hiring gets the right people on the bus, so does the selection of suppliers and others. Wherever possible the right "fit" in terms of behavioural values should be pursued when selecting partners.

It is also important that regular evaluations of partner relationships are undertaken. "Our" organization will have established a set of values that it is prepared to be judged against both internally and externally. These should form a central part of evaluation and assessment approaches with suppliers and to the degree possible customers. If issues arise where it is clear that a relationships is heading towards a toxic outcome, both parties must be willing to meet and address the problem.

No employee should have to suffer abuse or mistreatment at the hands of customers, suppliers, or any others. While management cannot act directly to deal with the problem, they must support members of the workforce who raise a problem, with the intent that someone needs to address it. Problems in relationships often show up as operational issues:

- Poor or misleading communications.
- Available information not being shared.
- Shifting blame for problems.
- Moving away from mutual benefit to win / lose thinking.
- "Bad mouthing" the partner organization.
- Rudeness to shared relationships (e.g., a sub-contract supplier of after-sales service who is rude to "your" customers).

These problems can "bleed back" into an organization if not addressed and resolved. If necessary the problem may need to be escalated to senior management of both organizations, so that it can be dealt with on an "inconsistent values" issue basis.

One other key area is relationships with "non operational" organizations such as regulators. Internally, the values must be understood to apply to all relationships that are part of the business model. The regulators have a job to do and if toxic relationships develop this can slow down activity and bias both working relationships and outcomes.

Honesty and reflectiveness are important in assessing external relationships.

Regulators sometimes develop toxic attitudes because they don't trust the organization they are dealing with. This may be based on past behaviour where they have been lied to or information has been withheld. The organization undergoing regulation must "first put its own house in order." It is impossible to have good regulatory relationships if the organization is behaving badly. This is exactly the same as trying to build a good culture internally when the reality of actions taken is unfair, unethical, and generally not responsible. So, first look in the mirror.

Convinced that the problem is not on the organization being regulated side, then efforts must be developed to build the foundation for a good relationship. One source suggests five qualities that are critical:

- Be transparent – no hidden agendas.
- Be clear – ensure communications are open and clear
- Be reliable – do what you say you will do. Commit and follow through.
- Be proactive – volunteer information (regulators and many other "partners' don't like surprises).
- Mutual respect – avoid being judgemental, accept that each is acting in good faith to do their job.

Toxic relationships with external parties are equally important with dysfunctional behaviour internally. Treating regulators as "the enemy" is never a winning strategy. Once again it is about balance. Each have a clear agenda, which is partly driven by self interest. After all, each organization has a functional purpose. But each will be better positioned to achieve their goals through collaboration and cooperation rather than an adversarial approach – especially one where it turns toxic.

11.5 Getting the wrong people off the bus

Eventually employees that exhibit toxic behaviour have to be removed from the workplace. If it is discovered that their "changed" behaviour has been caused by personal issues, then these need to be dealt with. This will include a leave of absence if necessary. If it turns out to be a "bad hire" then a mutually agreeable parting must be found – remembering that the remainder of the workforce are always looking to ensure the treatment of the individual is fair. If the problem is with a partner or external organization, then steps must be taken to change the interface; the person on one or both sides need to be transferred elsewhere.

The final situation comes down to "when you have tried everything" and the person has clearly arrived at a point where they will continue "to be a problem." Leaders cannot ignore the problem and must take steps to part company. Each problem will be situational and require a custom solution. Early retirement maybe. Geographic transfer.

When all options have been looked at, a parting of the ways must occur. This must be "fair in the circumstances." A financial arrangement can often be negotiated that provides a fair compensation. Whatever the root cause of the problem must be investigated but the individual MUST be removed. Transparency is important so others, to the highest degree possible can make an accurate assessment of fairness.

Retaining even one person who exhibits toxic behaviour in the workplace is a risk not worth taking. Some situations will be a challenge. The independent, highly intelligent researcher who thinks and acts as though everyone else is an idiot – and who has no empathy and no filter – so tells them that. He or she may be doing more damage than good.

The senior executive who "plays the game" and attends all the team building, harassment, and diversity workshops, but clearly disagrees with these things and continues to act like a "one man band" needs to be dealt with. It doesn't matter how senior or "important" the person is – their negative impact on the rest of the business must be minimized.

It can be highly rewarding for someone who can work with these individuals and coach and support them to become a "better person." This is what investing in your people is all about. But at some point the decision will need to be taken to either continue to work with them as they clearly understand the problems and are committed to working through them, or to "get them off the bus."

12 Fixing the people issue

Recognizing that organizations that are not balancing management and leadership, and either already have a toxic culture or a at risk of having mediocre results and may eventually drift towards one, what can be done?

The evolution of business towards being knowledge based and people intensive, requires a shift in strategic thinking. Traditional approaches to strategy have evolved with management of task being the prime focus. Now organizations need the same level of focus on planning the human aspects of performance. This is not a traditional HR management role.

Many existing approaches are built around HR having the responsibility to obtain and manage the human resources that were required for the business model. People morale and commitment is the responsibility of each manager and supervisor. HR can be advocate and advisor but the responsibility to build the culture rests with every single person in a leadership position. If an organization has a toxic culture, HR may have a role in it, but leadership is where the responsibility lies.

This is similar to the role that finance plays in obtaining capital to fund business operations. The traditional role of finance was to obtain the cash required to fund the business and putting in place systems and controls to track and monitor expenditures. Tracking and reporting all aspects of how the money came in and where it went was a core requirement. As the need for better financial information grew, the role of finance evolved to include the development and application of management accounting. This took financial people to the heart of planning and reporting. Financial decision making today sits at the heart of business strategy and execution.

HR professionals face the same opportunity to move from obtaining human resources, and tracking, managing, and monitoring their use to one of supporting management apply strategic thinking to people. This is the reality of making the words "people are our greatest asset" into a strategic reality, where people do indeed sit at the heart of an organizations strategy.

12.1 First there was management teaching
Management focuses on the task of creating the desired outcomes, through a structured approach

Business schools tend to teach management as a process, reflecting what has been discussed about the "management" aspect of a manager or supervisors job position. It is said that "In order to be an effective manager, one must be able to get the job done." Totally consistent with our focus on task – the job. There are four parts to the management process: planning, organizing, leading/ directing, and controlling. (See Figure 11-1)

In the planning stage, a manager determines how best to accomplish a set goal. During the organizing stage, he or she determines the best way to allocate resources to achieve the desired goal. Typically, the desired goal of each manager is one or more outputs; these, combined together create the organizations desired outcomes.

The directing / leading stage involves the manager motivating and directing employees to work toward the goal. This is the area where traditional approaches to "people skills" was needed – as a sub-set of management skills and the management process. Today this role must evolve in parallel to the management process NOT as a sub-set.

The controlling stage requires the manager to evaluate and monitor their progress. This stage is focused on ensuring that things are being done as planned and in making changes when necessary. The whole management process is iterative in that this last stage of monitoring and evaluating feeds back into the first step of planning. The management process if often depicted as follows:

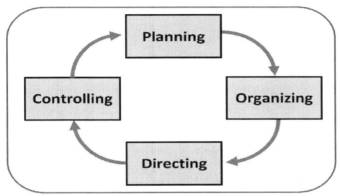

Figure 12-1 Traditional management approach

Since this model was created, the management role related to task has matured. Key milestones in the evolution impacting a managers task included:

- The development of management models to better understand the various underlying resources needed to be integrated to achieve task (discussed earlier e.g., models for excellence).
- The evolution and development of TQM (Total Quality Management) where the need for integration across and between the role and activities of different managers (cross functional work), started to be seen as an "integrated system."
- The maturing of process management that enhanced the capability of process control using tools such as SPC.

- The challenges of continuous improvement and creating a learning organization, where process improvement makes its way back into planning

These developments in the management of process, increasingly demonstrated that people considerations needed to be embedded within each step. The development of teamwork and quality circles and all sorts of other steps to better engage the workforce were implemented.

12.2 Then there was total system management
This evolution of people considerations led to a change to the management process model of planning, organizing, directing and control into a system based framework, now applied broadly based on the following model.

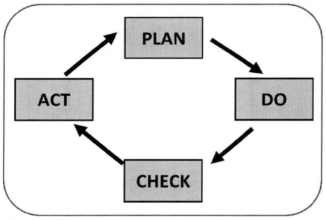

Figure 12-2 Deming / Shewhart model

This model – referred to as either the PDCA or PDSA (Study) framework is widely accepted as a foundation for business management. The original model was created by American physicist Walter A. Shewhart but gained prominence from the work of Dr William Edwards Deming as part of the "quality revolution" initially in Japanese manufacturing and then in the US and globally.

The management "task" responsibility within the model still reflects the four original steps, but the context is now at the enterprise level, and the leadership of the parallel people aspects must have equivalent attention.

Organizations planned (PLAN) what was needed, took steps to execute the plans (DO), put in place monitoring systems (CHECK) and then responded based on the information from the checking (ACT). This is the foundation of continual improvement. Within all four steps, all of the resources required for the business model are considered. The financial resources needed, the human resources, the capital equipment, the customers, and the suppliers.

What has all this got to do with culture and creating an integrated approach to building a people-centric strategy?

12.3 A base for common language and thinking.

An example of how pervasive "people strategy" needs to be can by thought of by comparing past approaches to process development to the need for an integrated human approach.

Many organizations have become obsessed with and committed to the need for process control and consistency. One example was the broad based adoption of an approach called 6 Sigma. The foundational thinking around this approach was that if processes were not planned and managed effectively, then outputs would lack control and unplanned variations and results would occur.

Organizations adopted statistical approaches to understand variation and demonstrate the impact that a lack of planning and control has on output. What was needed was a higher level of predictability of process performance. The following chart and its terminology became broadly adopted.

SIGMA level	Errors in judgement per million actions / decisions	Sigma "competitive" Rating	Potential risk of unplanned or unexpected behavior leading to loss
2	308,537	Non-competitive	High risk
3	66,807		Medium to high risk
4	6,210	Industry average	Medium risk
5	233		Low risk
6	3.4	World class	Almost zero risk

Figure 12-3 Six Sigma applied to interactions / relationships

The 6 Sigma statistical approach demonstrates that at a world class performance level, processes can perform at a level where predictability of output is high. Figure 10-3 shows that at 6 sigma (the bottom row), one can expect 3.4 errors per million transactions. Industry average is between 3 and 4 sigma – with the numbers of unplanned errors ranging from between 6,210 and 66,807 errors per million transaction.

Now imagine this approach on variation of outputs, applied to interactions between people, where relationships are important. How often do people talk to one another, or pass information or instructions? How often are people asked to make a decision, where either they are not sure of the procedures and don't know what action to take? How about someone who is just "having a bad day?" Add into this the complexity of different personalities and the variation of emotional responses. Every time there is a human interaction it is a "moment of truth." A point at which all the underlying values will be demonstrated or ignored.

Instead of looking at process variation, figure 10-3 actually applies 6 Sigma thinking to interactions between people. Exactly those transactions that are based on relationships. Think of the millions of time human interactions takes place between members of the workforce – internally and externally. Is it predictable? What steps have been taken to improve predictability and avoid problems and surprises? If an organizations workforce and the relationships are operating between three and four sigma, the likelihood is that there is a medium to high risk of a toxic culture developing. After all, its' unplanned. One can hope that people act they way they should, but what is the foundation for managing this, such that the risk of unplanned human behaviour is being understood and managed?

Can, and should an organization do something to try and reduce the behavioural variation whenever there are human interactions? Would this be of benefit to the organization? If the conclusion is that human interactions and the impact that have on behaviour internally are important then some sort of approach is needed. Is the same true externally with the impact of human behaviour on external relationships? Again, if the answer is positive, then a strategic approach to culture is needed.

Once an organization agrees that it needs to manage its' culture to enhance and improve the predictability of human performance in the same way that process performance has been addressed, then there needs to be a strategic approach, pervasive across all human aspects of the business – in the same way that 6 Sigma was pervasive across all process areas.

Some may know from experience that broad based; organization wide investments were made in 6 Sigma process improvement. Common terminology was used, such as the DMAIC approach. 6 Sigma was broadly understood as a concept. Executives were "on board" with the concept, approach, and investment. Steering groups, corporate strategy groups and improvement teams were developed. Internal specialists were trained in depth about the concepts involved and the approaches used. Metrics were developed to ensure that cause and effect relationships from improvements were understood and delivered.

What if this sort of broad based strategic thinking around "all things related to process" would be applied with the same rigour to all things related to human relationships and interactions?

12.4 Building culture into strategy

Organizational goals and objectives are typically weighted towards the achievement of task – the "what do we want to do" aspects. These typically focus on outcomes such as volumes, profits, market share, growth rates and similar aspects of "<u>what</u> we do."

With the growing concern around corporate brand, reputation and behaviour, organizations also need to consider "how we do what we do." What does our behaviour need to look like to sustain and grow our reputation and image in the market place? Additionally, if INTERNAL behaviour is to be a strategic competitive advantage, then it also needs to be built into the PDCA model.

Many organizations are already making many of the investments required that form part of a strategic plan for culture. Sadly, for many these are "events" and not part of a bigger integrated strategic approach.

As an example, investments in training and development, especially related to areas like team development, problem solving, and leadership training are consuming significant resources – but rather than being part of a broad, outcome oriented strategy, they are approached piecemeal. Often the content and approaches are not aligned nor are they integrated with areas like organizational values and the culture desired. There is no common strategy. No common foundation of expectations. No common link to peoples personality.

The discipline of using something like the DMAIC approach, is not present in human and relationship management in most organizations. How could it be used? As a starting point information could be tracked around disciplinary actions, complaints, accidents, turnover, time off for sickness

– especially longer term disability for mental health issues. (After all, can employees be subject to PTSD – like service people in a war zone?)

In developing an approach to human relationships, the model might be used in the following manner:

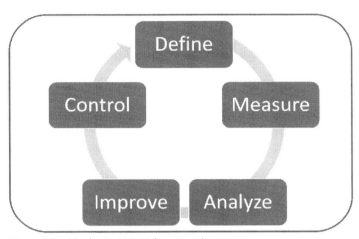

Figure 12-4 The basic DMAIC framework

DEFINE would refer to the need for a strategic discussion on what is the issue. Is human behaviour inconsistent? What are the problems? What are the issues being seen? (Does the organization even have a structured human capital metrics program that ties to behavioural expectations?)

MEASURE would come from initiating some data collection – even using existing information such as disputes, problems, complaints, non-conformances, scores on feedback assessments, and input from third parties.

ANALYZE would focus on why these problems and issues were occurring. The goal is to define root causes so that the symptoms are not addressed but the underlying issues.

IMPROVE would be the stage where the highest priority root causes were looked into and policies, procedures or other aspects changed.

MEASURE would be to compare the "event count" metrics at the beginning of the improvement project with the results after the changes occurred to ensure that the action taken has resulted in improvement.

Figure 11-5 illustrates what embedding strategic thinking into the PDCA process would look like. The PDCA remains the same but the process / task activity that supports the "what," is complemented by the human strategy that deals with the "how." The behaviours that will drive positive relationships and sustain a positive culture.

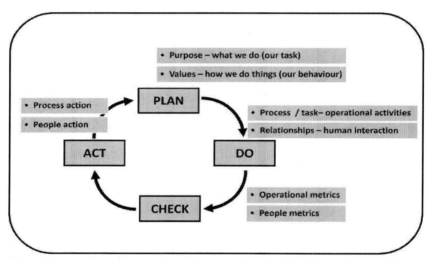

Figure 12-5 People and Process together

Typically, at the planning stage, an environmental scan is undertaken, and the strategies adopted reflect the reality of the market as well as the workplace. This is the stage where the desired behaviour that supports both the brand and reputation as well as the "way we want to do things around here" are considered. This is a critical stage in making sure that the organization observes and accommodates changing social expectations. As an example, society is ramping up its focus on diversity, equity, and inclusion (DE&I).

Organizations need to understand any legislation that demands mandatory compliance PLUS consider "societal" changes, that if not reflected will have a negative impact – demonstrating the organization is out of touch. From a risk management perspective, if this activity is not effectively carried out the organizations governance framework will be at risk. This step related to human capital is also the stage where the board must be involved and commit to the considerations related to human capital.

Step	Purpose strategy	People strategy
Plan	What do we have to do to achieve our stated business purpose? Mission / Vision, goals	How to we have to behave to be responsible and competitive. Values / behaviours
Do	Planning and execution of business projects, processes, tasks and activities, including alignment with people strategies.	Planning and execution of HR systems and supports and leadership development to support business processes.
Check	Development of operational metrics – inputs, process, output and outcomes.	Development of human capital metrics – inputs, processes, outputs and outcomes.
Act	Review of results against plans and adjust.	Review of actual versus planned behaviour and adjust.

Each step follows the PDCA model. A key aspect is the parallel consideration of task and behaviour at each stage. Very often toxic cultures develop because there are no metrics being used that focus on outputs and outcomes. Traditionally many HR metrics being used are focused on compliance issues such as hiring of minorities, health and safety and HR process activities such as the time required to fill positions. There is nothing that feeds back to people strategy.

The development of progressive HR metrics will play an important role in linking people approaches and actual performance back to strategy. Each stage can be expanded into understanding the people and process aspects.

13 Fixing the corporate issue

The behaviour of corporate entities within society has been a matter of discussion and concern as long as they have existed. Unethical behaviour by people investing in and running "businesses" has always existed.

Frameworks for corporate governance evolve as society changes, with the goal of continuing to ensure transparency and accountability. However, while many legal and regulatory aspects of change have gradually been implemented, there is also a parallel effort, mainly on a voluntary basis to try and incorporate more "self accountability" into corporate activity. Some of these have linkages to changes in mandatory reporting requirements but many remain optional. Three important areas of development are:

- Integrated reporting – including the evolution from the triple bottom line, through to corporate social responsibility and integrated thinking.
- ESG – embracing integration and multiple "capitals," and the creation of the International Sustainability Standards Board (ISSB)
- Corporate Purpose as adopted by the business round table of CEO's.

Each of these are efforts to bring more accountability and responsibility to businesses as members of society. Are they working to address the issues of behaviour and the human and societal aspects? Will they help identify risk associated with toxic culture? If the evolution of transparency and accountability is keeping pace, it will be helping investors, regulators and others evaluate the health of "the system."

13.1 Integrated Reporting

Almost fifty years ago a movement started for corporate social responsibility (CSR), founded on the ideas of the "social contract." Social contract was the concept that established the idea that business should embrace business ethics and a responsiveness to societal stakeholders.

CSR grew and morphed through various stages including the triple bottom line. This developed in parallel to the evolution of business models, including the frameworks for excellence and TQM (Total Quality Management). Performance measurement and reporting changes developed including the balanced scorecard[3], and corporate dashboards. External reporting frameworks developed including GRI (Global Reporting Institute).

Many organizations adopted ideas of broader based corporate reporting and accountability, producing supplemental annual reports to complement their traditional financial statements. These supplemental reports were optional although non-financial "audit opinions" were sometimes provided.

In 2012 the idea of integrating traditional financial reports with these supplemental reports was suggested, and the IIRC (International Integrated Reporting Council) was formed. In 2013 they proposed a framework of six "capitals" upon which reports would be based. These capitals included financial, manufactured, natural, intellectual, human and social / relationship.

This gave hope to many, especially those concerned about organizational behaviour and the human aspects, that this step would start to form a core

---

[3] Kaplan and Norton

component of accountability. This might give investors an insight into both the size and impact of human capital but also the health. It also gave hope that the link between the large investments being made in developing "the human aspects of the workplace" would be recognized and linked back to the value of human capital in some way. As such it was possible that there could be indicators related to risk of a toxic culture developing.

While the overall IIRC framework, referred to as <IR> was adopted by many and offered a great "learning framework" around the integrated nature of resources used in an organizations business model, two problems developed. Financial reports remained separate, following existing accounting and reporting standards and few if any connections were made between financial information and the remaining five capitals.

Additionally, the major focus on greater transparency and accountability was primarily on natural capital – mirroring the growing global concern over climate change and global warming and the need for business activity to address improving operations to lower environmental impact. Little attention was paid to the other capitals. While some organizations expanded disclosure of "people topics" there was almost no financial linkage, and reports were biased towards traditional compliance areas. A few did report on employee engagement. Almost none discussed the role of leadership.

While this approach offered the potential for a broad based, societal approach to corporate performance, it was seen by many as an added burden to business. In 2021 the IIRC was amalgamated with the US based Sustainability Accounting Standards Board (SASB) to form the Value Reporting Foundation[xxii] (VRF). SASB had been established to develop standards for all non-financial aspects of US financial and regulatory reporting. SASB was strong in climate change issues and had some level of focus on human capital, but these were heavily related to existing compliance, with areas such as employee health and safety; employee diversity, inclusion, and engagement; and labour practices – many of which have existing statutory requirements.

This creation of the VRF retained and promoted the six capital framework of the IIRC. For many this and using the words "Value Foundation" raised the positive impression that maybe it was being realized that investor value was the result of the combined capitals – not just financial capital. Maybe the importance of people as the largest consumer of cash, but also the key component of value creation would increase in prominence.

After all, the case was already being made that there was an impact on business value from a toxic culture. Barings Bank failed. ENRON failed. Carillion failed. The stock value of Activision Blizzard stock fell 30% in September 2021 when the sexual misconduct suits were filed. It didn't destroy the company but facilitated the purchase by Microsoft. The list could go on. All of these one way or another linked to behaviour.

Maybe efforts would now accelerate to build the bridge between the expenditure of financial capital to acquire, create and sustain the value of an organizations other capitals. Maybe the issue of an effective or toxic culture would start to be linked to financial reporting as well as non-financial metrics. Sadly, this idea appeared wrong as the next amalgamation rolled out.

13.2 ESG and the ISSB

Shortly after the amalgamation of the IIRC and SASB into the VRF, another amalgamation was announced leading to a new international standards organization. The VRF was folded into the International Accounting Standards Foundation. Prior to adding the VRF, the main activity of the foundation was to oversee the work of the International Accounting Standards Board (IASB).

The existing mandate of IASB to develop global accounting standards remained, but a new board called the International Sustainability

Standards Board[xxiii] (ISSB) was created to focus on non-financial reporting standards. The new foundation still promotes the concept of the six capitals IIRC <IR> framework, as well as the integrated thinking approach; it also embraced the existing work and standards developed by SASB.

The main driver for these amalgamations was a desire for simplicity and clarity of reporting requirements. On the face of it, bringing together financial and non-financial reporting standards under a single body had merit. Time will tell whether this combination will be the final step in true, broad based integrated reporting, with adequate coverage given to all the aspects of an organizations business model. A model which after all determines both the investors value, as well as the ability to deliver and sustain earnings.

Two problems are apparent. Firstly, the accounting profession has not shown creativity in addressing the lack of disclosure related to financial expenditures to build and create intangible infrastructure – the very essence of four of the other five capitals – most importantly disclosures around human capital.

Secondly, there is the issue of materiality. Deciding what is important enough to be included in the reporting. Accounting has long focused on materiality as being defined by the investors view. However, the evolution of non-financial reporting, particularly outside the US and predominantly in Europe, has focused on a stakeholder view. Statements by the ISSB appear to indicate that their single shareholder focus will remain. This does not bode well for a shift to broad based integrated reporting that includes adequate attention to people issues and in particular organizational culture.

The conclusion seems to be at this stage, that relying on statutory reporting to "make public" issues impacting organizational culture will be a low, if not non-existent priority. Little insight will be provided into the impact of the organization on society, especially in terms of the human aspects. The traditional shareholder and investor view of the world will prevail.

One is left wondering whether the current "push back" on ESG reporting is a comment on the inadequacy of the approach to address the need for transparency and accountability. This lack of comprehensive coverage as well as some who practise "greenwashing" could easily explain the reluctance to spend the time and effort on looking at this information?

13.3 Organizational Purpose.

On the 19th of August 2019, the Business Roundtable in the USA, announced the release of a new Statement on the Purpose of a Corporation[xxiv] signed by 181 CEOs (there are now more on the website) who committed to lead their companies for the benefit of all stakeholders – customers, employees, suppliers, communities, and shareholders. Since 1997 the roundtable had endorsed principles of shareholder primacy – that corporations exist principally to serve shareholders.

Within this statement the comment on "employees" was as follows:

- *Investing in our employees. This starts with compensating them fairly and providing important benefits. It also includes supporting them through training and education that help develop new skills for a rapidly changing world. We foster diversity and inclusion, dignity, and respect.*

This new mantra "the purpose of the corporation" has become a rallying call for CEO's to position the performance of their organization from a broader perspective. But one is left feeling that people are still seen mainly as resources. There is no call for "fostering an inclusive workplace" although there is a commitment to engage with shareholders. There is a commitment to foster diversity, inclusion, dignity, and respect. But "fostering it" and building a workplace based on the foundation of these topics is quite different. We have seen that statutory reporting is biased towards compliance. Discussions of future SEC "people guidelines" appear also to be focused on compliance.

It is also interesting that these "progressive" CEO's who signed the statement, seem to be out of step with the reporting focus which apparently looks at shareholders as the prime area when assessing materiality. A December 2020 Harvard paper[xxv] seemed to clearly suggest that the promises made in the Round Table statement were more PR that substance.

As a statement in the Harvard Business Review said, shortly after the BRT release its purpose statement, under the headline, "Is the Business Roundtable Statement Just Empty Rhetoric?" the writer suggests that *"for many of the BRT signatories, truly internalizing the meaning of their words would require rethinking their whole business."* Is this window dressing – the equivalent of greenwashing or will there be REAL disclosure and real change that provides far greater insight into the risk of human behaviour on the value and sustainability of the organization?

Research behind the 2020 report mentioned in the previous paragraph revealed that "rethinking their whole business" really didn't happen. A Fortune article commenting on the Harvard 2020 report quoted *"Especially noteworthy are the study's findings regarding shareholder proposals and how companies responded to them. At 27 of the signatory companies, shareholders requested votes on proposals to implement the principles in the statement. In about half the cases, the companies sought permission from the Security and Exchange Commission to deny the vote. For all the proposals that went to a vote, the researchers find, 'the company invariably recommended that shareholders vote against them.'"*

After all, as many point out, these are the CEO's whose pay packets dwarf the take home pay of most members of the workforce, creating an underlying concern about fairness. Restating corporate purpose does not re-frame an organization into becoming a responsible business from societies perspective.

13.4 The real challenge

The real problem is twofold – either leaders "just don't get it" or the organizations they run are so large and complex, that any problems with behaviour are either hidden, or people lie about it, or it never makes it to a leadership level that is capable of doing anything about it. Understand toxic cultures don't just happen. Events occur that if not dealt with fester and grow larger.

The issue of telling the truth is critical. There is an incorrect assumption that an effective organization is one that is open enough, that people can tell the truth without fear. This is only part of the problem. If the truth is being told but not heard or acted upon, the fact that people are saying it means nothing.

If toxic culture is to be driven out of the workplace it requires an absolute focus on leadership. Starting with a board and investors that recognize the linkage between managing BOTH the task as well as the culture. That clearly define BOTH the expected operational purpose – the desired business outcomes but also the desired behavioural outcomes.

It requires leadership at the highest level to be fundamentally committed to both:

a) the underlying principles of *what the organization needs to do operationally* to deliver on the desired business purpose and outcomes, through clear strategies, goals, objectives, and strategies.

b) What the organization is required to do, to deliver on the *expected behaviours* in terms of organizational values, supported by clear strategies, goals, objectives, and strategies

It requires leaders who go out and seek the truth – who are "in touch" enough to be able to discern reality. Some organizations put in place culture change groups – independent groups of "activists" who are supported by management, have credibility with the workforce and can act as a sounding board for leaders.

Another option is to develop the equivalent of "Culture black-belts." People who are professionally trained in areas such as conflict resolution and understanding human behaviour and who can work as coaches with managers. They can be called in by anyone in the organization where reality is not reflecting intent. IT is not about statements, meetings, policies, or procedures – but about ACTION – doing things differently.

Statements by CEO's who publicly commit to running their businesses considering all stakeholders, run hollow when subsequent changes in any governance frameworks are non-existent.

The reality is that for the time being the importance of toxic culture to the health of any business model will be something that falls into the "optional disclosure" area. Leaders and boards should be driving this reporting internally – even if the market place has not yet caught up with reality. Boards should be asking "what is our strategic approach to culture?" and "how is management embedding our values and expectations into everyday business activity?" Plus of course "how do you know its working?"

Without a good oversight and governance model, surprises caused by toxic cultures will continue. Performance will be impaired and solutions may do more damage than good.

Corporate Culture

14 Sober second thought

Real change, and the idea of organizations being valued members of society for both what they produce, the jobs they create and the way that they behave. Is it a "bridge too far," an unrealistic dream? Does the current "push back" on ESG reporting signal an unwillingness to change?

Are ethics and free enterprise capitalism impossible partners? Does business have to succeed by avoiding morality and just focusing on legality? Is win / lose the mantra of success, rather than seeking win / win even if it requires longer negotiations and compromises?

Is it possible, in the reality of existing business models to succeed based on the service, quality, innovation and cost competitiveness of products and services or is manipulation required – cutting corners and taking advantage of others? Are wages going to always be set by the lowest common denominator? Is a "living wage" incompatible with seeking the lowest cost of every business input including labour? Is tax avoidance with its social implications going to remain unchallenged?

If business is to change and be seen as responsible, the foundation of change will be a different approach to how they operate. History has allowed the workforce and management relationship to be adversarial, yet studies in the past have shown a correlation between non-adversarial relationships and business success. Organizations like Just Capital and The B Lab / B The Change are attempting to provide a forum, tools, help and guidance to leaders who are seeking to generate real change.

But at the end of the day, change will only happen if the governance of business organizations is led by boards and senior executives that are committed to the success of their enterprises but based on not compromising on their social contract. Not abusing any partners involved in providing resources to their business model. Not taking advantage of the free market for their own ends alone without considering the impact on society.

This willingness to change might be considered a problem if past experience is any indicator. The Business Roundtable public statement and commitment appears to be currently signed by 262 executives. In spite of recommendations many years ago that, to improve corporate governance the role of Chairman and CEO be split, almost 50% of the signatories to the "Purpose" statement still hold the joint title. Seems that REALLY changing is difficult.

It IS a difficult challenge. It is often far easier to limit or reduce payrolls and to lay off staff, than to question whether the business model itself, is the root cause of competitive issues. To take advantage and leverage suppliers knowing that they have few options other than to "buckle under." To ignore problem employees or problem customers hoping that eventually they will just go away.

The business enterprise of the 21st century poses harsh challenges – not just because of global competition and the pace of change, but because its' foundation is now human capital. People are not an amorphous collection of generic resources. They are hard to lead. Hard to manage. Hard to predict actions and behaviours. People are the greatest challenge internally but also watch, listen, hear, and judge corporate activity externally. People are prone to jumping to conclusions without all the facts. To reacting or acting impetuously and emotionally without cool, hard consideration and evaluation. THAT is the reality that leadership faces in todays organizations.

> **One of the greatest losses in the world is the loss of human potential created through poor leadership.**

Business leaders who are able to build cultures where people are treated like partners and recognized and rewarded for their contribution will open up strategic potential and advantage. The faster change occurs the more important it will be for people to trust their leaders and through this, to shorten the time frame necessary to shift and adapt to these changes.

> **Most people don't resist change. They resist being told to change especially by others who they don't trust.**

Leaders who see "people" as difficult, and like sheep who need to be told what to do and when to do it, might find "leadership with people" more of a challenge than traditional directing and controlling. Being a trusted, respected, and credible leader of people will be frustrating, and challenging. But the new business model demands that a foundation around behaviour must rank equally to that of the organizations task, purpose, and mission.

Only by seeking a new way for the business model to work – a new way to better integrate all the resources for optimum performance, will the challenge of a toxic culture be eliminated.

Focusing on "purpose" seems like re-arranging the deck chairs on the Titanic. Every business has always had a purpose which forms a foundation of strategic planning. It is the SOCIETAL Purpose that needs renewal and revival. A new focus that balances BOTH corporate and social purpose is needed, with people seen as enablers.

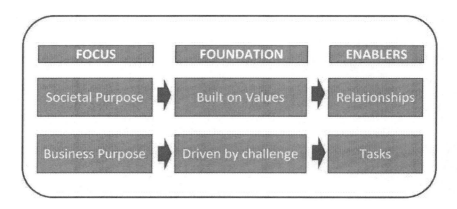

Purpose remains a core aspect of an organizations governance model. Why are we here? What is our role in society as an attractive investment as well as a creator of economic activity – jobs, buying goods and services, providing benefits back to society. Also, our purpose to provide products or services to other members of society. These must be the focus – purpose is not single dimension.

To achieve "the purpose" the foundations must be both what we do and how we behave while we do it – internally and externally. In a people-centric environment the aspect of human behaviour becomes paramount and must be seen as equally important to "getting the job done."

Finally, the enablers of achieving the purpose. Relationships, both internally and externally are the basis of the business model. A model that acquires the needed resources and weaves them together to create value and to deliver results.

The Responsible Business of the 21st century provides value to society and to its shareholders. It acts morally and ethically. It creates and sustains a business model where integrity, honesty and ethical behaviour are considered equally important as growth, profits, and dividends.

Toxic culture has no place in a 21st century business. Leaders who fail to recognize they have a problem, or fail to act on the problem, or fail to develop a risk management approach to ensure that culture is managed and not left to chance, will face a higher risk of failure. Of having the curtains pulled back like the Wizard of OZ only to have it revealed that leadership was in name only. It IS a choice – but one where if taken with all its' challenges will create and sustain the organizations of the future.

Corporate Culture

15 Bibliography

Becker, Brian. E., Huselid, Mark. A., and Ulrich, F. Dave (2001) *The HR scorecard,* Harvard Business Press.

Blanchard, Ken, and O'Connor, Michael (1997) *Managing by Values*, Berrett-Koehler.

Campanella, Jack (1999) *Principles of Quality Costs, 3rd edition*, Quality Press, ASQ.

Cohen, Ben, and Warwick, Mal (2006) *Values Driven Business*, Berrett-Koehler.

Crosby, Phil (1979) *Quality is Free*, Signet.

Edvinsson, L., and Malone. M. S. (1997) *Intellectual Capital*, pp.168–169, Harper Business.

Fitz-enz, Jac (2000) *The ROI of Human Capital*, AMACOM.

Gleeson-White, Jane (2014) *Six Capitals: The Revolution Capitalism has to have – or can accountants save the planet*, Allen & Unwin.

Higgins, Jamie Fiore, (2022), *Bully Market: My Story of Money and Misogyny at Goldman Sachs*, Simon & Schuster

Hood, Daniel (2019) *Trust is just the beginning*, Accounting Today (Study from ACCA, IFAC, and CA ANZ), March 4.

IFAC (2015) *Materiality in Integrated Reporting*, Integrated Reporting <IR> and International Federation of Accountants.

IIRC (2013) *The International <IR> Framework*, International Integrated Reporting Council, December.

Johnson, Thomas. H., and Kaplan, Robert, S. (1987) *Relevance Lost: The Rise and Fall of Management Accounting*, Harvard Business School Press.

Kaplan, Robert. S., and Norton, David. P. (1996) *The Balanced Scorecard*, Harvard Business Review Press.

Kaplan, Robert. S., and Norton, David. P. (2006) *Alignment*, Harvard Business School Publishing.

Kearns. P., and Woollard, Stuart (2019) *The Mature Corporation*, Cambridge Scholars Press.

Lev, Baruch, and Gu, Feng (2016) *The End of Accounting*, Wiley.

Liker, Jeffrey. K. (2011) *Toyota Under Fire: How Toyota faced the challenges of the recall and came out stronger*, McGraw Hill.

Liker, Jeffrey. K. (2004) *The Toyota Way*, McGraw Hill.

Liker, Jeffrey. K., and Hoseus, Michael (2008) *Toyota Culture: The Heart and Soul of the Toyota Way*, McGraw Hill.

Liker, Jeffrey. K., and Meier, David. P. (2007) *Toyota Talent; Developing Your People the Toyota Way*, McGraw Hill.

Magee, David (2007) *How Toyota Became #1*, Portfolio.

Nayar, Vineet (2010) *Employees First, Customers Second*, Harvard Business Press.

Pasternack, Bruce. A., Viscio, Albert. J., (1998), *The Centerless Corporation, A new model for transforming your organization for growth and prosperity,* Simon and Schuster

Peters, Sandra (2020) *FASB Turns Up the Heat on Goodwill Impairment Testing*, CFA Institute, February 12.

Rother, Mike (2010) *Toyota Kata*, McGraw Hill.

Schmidt, Eric., and Rosenberg, Jonathan (2014) *How Google Works*, Hachette Book Group Ltd.

Shepherd, N. (2005) *Governance, Accountability and Sustainable Development: An agenda for the 21st century*, Thomson Carswell, Canada.

Shepherd, N., and Adams, M. (2014) *Unrecognized Intangible Assets: Identification, Management and Reporting*, Statements in Management Accounting series, Institute of Management Accountants.

Shepherd, N. (2021) *How Accountants Lost their Balance*, Kindle Direct Publishing (Eduvision / Jannas Publications).

Shepherd, N. (2021) *Corporate Culture – Combining Purpose and Values*, Kindle Direct Publishing (Eduvision / Jannas Publications).

Shepherd, B. (2021) *The Cost of Poor Culture: The massive financial opportunity in an enhanced workplace culture,* Jannas Publications / Kindle Direct publishing.

Smyth, Peter, and Shepherd. N. (2012) *Reflective Leaders and High-Performance Organizations*, iUniverse Publishing.

Stewart, T. (1997) *Intellectual Capital: The New Wealth of organizations*, pp. 232–233, Doubleday.

Stewart, Tom (1997) *Intellectual Capital: The New Wealth of Nations*, Currency Doubleday.

Wallis, Jim (2010) *Rediscovering Values*, Simon & Schuster.

Weiss, David. S. (2000) *High Performance HR – Leveraging Human Resources for Competitive Advantage*, John Wiley.

Corporate Culture

Nick has over 50 years of varied work experience including senior general management and finance roles. From 1989 to 2018 he was active in his own management consulting and professional development company. Currently he still spends time on research and writing, that focuses in the areas of organizational sustainability, human capital, and integrated reporting. Nick has experience working in, and with private family business, public corporations, and governments and NPO's, both in Canada and internationally.

Nick is co-author of "Reflective Leaders and High-Performance Organizations" written in 2012 with Dr. Peter Smyth. Nick also wrote "Governance, Accountability and Sustainable Development" (2005), the "Controllers Handbook" (2008) and since retirement in late 2017 has written a number of additional books related to organizational culture and human aspects of business. Nick lives with his wife at an old 1923 log cabin, west of Ottawa, Ontario that sits close to the Ottawa river.

Contact Nick at nick@eduvision.ca

16 End Notes

While the bibliography provides a number of publications that the reader might enjoy that give direct or indirect but relevant information to this book, there are other sources contained in magazines website and articles hat may also help.

The following endnotes contain these additional references. Note that the web references were valid as of October 2022 but might have changed since.

---

[i] **The Great resignation**
It may be considered simplistic to connect a toxic culture and the great resignation – but the reality is that people have had a chance to try a different work model. Not just for personal reasons but because it can provide a better balance to and control over life and it avoids the climate impacts of commuting.

[ii] **What is driving the great resignation**
The article from MITSloan magazine, Jan 11th, 2002 "Toxic Culture Is Driving the Great Resignation" provides some useful insight.
https://sloanreview.mit.edu/article/toxic-culture-is-driving-the-great-resignation/

[iii] **The other two books on Corporate Culture.**
The two books are in the bibliography – "Corporate Culture" was written to explain the methods we used in our consulting practise, that helped organizations address their values and behaviour. The second book "The Cost of Poor Culture" demonstrates "where the money goes" and the financial risks and losses caused by a poor or toxic culture,

[iv] **Carillion and the Parliamentary Committee**
This failure was an interesting case and is worth more research if the reader has time. It seems to bring together many problems – not just the toxic culture issues but the failure of "checks and balances" including the complete failure of the annual financial audit to highlight any risk or impending problems. These very public issues have an impact on people's "belief" in business integrity.
https://www.theguardian.com/business/2018/may/16/mps-dole-out-the-blame-over-carillions-collapse

[v] **Toxic workplaces – HRPA**

HRPA and most international HR support areas provide a great deal of good information on toxic workplace. This May 12th, 2021 article "Tackling a Toxic Work Culture" provides some great insights into what the problem is and how to start looking at it.
https://www.hrpa.ca/hr-insights/tackling-a-toxic-work-culture/

[vi] **The FAANG group of organizations**

Those interested in investing will recognize the grouping used of the FAANG stocks – Facebook, Amazon, Apple, Netflix, and Google. What is important about these companies and others like them is that a substantial portion of investor value is tied up in what are know as intangibles. Central and critical to these are relationships.
https://www.businessinsider.com/personal-finance/what-is-faang

[vii] **The Centerless Corporation**

Readers may want to access this book which is included in the bibliography. Its' value is that although it was written in 1998 it clearly presented the reality that organizations would have to become people-centric in order to compete in the future knowledge economy.
https://www.simonandschuster.com/books/The-Centerless-Corporation/Bruce-A-Pasternack/9780684851990

[viii] **Gallup Q12 Meta-analysis**

The bibliography includes a book titled "First Break all the Rules," by Buckingham and Coffman. Much of the content of this book links to the annual report produced by Gallup. According to their website "the largest study of its kind to date -- examines decades of employee engagement and performance data from more than 100,000 teams to evaluate the connection between employee engagement and 11 key business outcomes."
https://www.gallup.com/workplace/321725/gallup-q12-meta-analysis-report.aspx

[ix] **The Cost of Poor Culture**

This book, listed in the biography is based on a similar approach to understand the costs of poor quality. In the quality revolution of the 1970's and 80's many boards, CEO's and senior management thought quality was about compliance. It was only when they realized the major negative financial impact that poor quality was having on performance that they started to invest in "prevention" to reduce previously unrecognized and bred failure costs.

[x] **New York Federal Reserve initiative on culture**

The banking and financial services industry has been "in the eye of the storm" when it comes to poor culture. In a progressive approach, the NY Federal Reserve believe that culture (and effective governance) is at the foundation of behaviour in these industries, and as a result has been sponsoring extensive research in the area and promoting reform. As indicated before "it starts at the top."
https://www.newyorkfed.org/governance-and-culture-reform

[xi] **MIT Sloan – Toxic behaviour and the great resignation**
While many believe that the problem of getting people back to work is financially driven, this article demonstrates that it is a culture issue more than anything else.
https://sloanreview.mit.edu/article/toxic-culture-is-driving-the-great-resignation/

[xii] **Cost to UK economy of sickness and health in the workplace**
As an example, the societal costs of ill health attributed to the workplace can be significant. These costs are often referred to as "externalities" because the impact is created by business – but business does not directly pay the costs.
https://www2.deloitte.com/content/dam/Deloitte/uk/Documents/life-sciences-health-care/deloitte-uk-foph-role-of-employers.pdf

[xiii] **BBC investigation by Equality and Human Rights Commission**
This report demonstrates how hard it is for an organization to position itself with a positive culture.
https://www.equalityhumanrights.com/en/our-work/news/investigation-equal-pay-bbc-makes-recommendations-rebuild-trust-female-employees

[xiv] **The Boeing saga**
There are many articles and reports about the Boeing 737 saga as well as a host of legal materials from the hearings and investigations. The MIT Culture 500 is a good resource for following professed "values" underlying culture with actual performance.
https://sloanreview.mit.edu/culture500/company/c181/Boeing

[xv] **Paul Stern, Nortel CEO**
Paul Stern was CEO of Nortel from 1989 – 1992. A case study produced by the Rotman School of Business at the University of Toronto stated, "The appointment of an outsider as the new leader was resented by Nortel's senior executives. Within a few months, half of the two dozen senior corporate staff departed. Nortel staff said they found Paul Stern's management style to be autocratic and felt it was unsettling for employees. They also found that some of his actions were sudden and abrupt, leading to confusion and low morale among staff and further contributing to the attrition of senior executives." In short he came in and destroyed the culture.
https://www.rotman.utoronto.ca/-/media/Files/Programs-and-Areas/CanadianBusinessHistory/Nortel_November2011_5.pdf

[xvi] **Fearless Culture**
While the quote comes from an individual who runs a culture consulting organization it reflects the reality of the problem when it comes to leadership. The link to his 202 article is below.
https://www.fearlessculture.design/blog-posts/narcissistic-leaders-destroy-culture-from-within

[xvii] **The 3 basic motivation theories**
I have always liked Maslow because it seems to make sense – but the others are also valid / interesting. There are lots of sources for information. Here is a starting point.

https://www.managementstudyguide.com/classical-theories-of-motivation.htm
^{xviii} **ISO 10010:2022 Quality culture**
From "day one" those trying to implement work practices that enhanced process, stressed the importance of employee involvement. Finally, after almost thirty years, TC 176 who wrote the quality standard released this supplemental guide.
https://www.iso.org/standard/38457.html

^{xix} **Lumina Learning**
This UK based company is at the leading edge of tools to support and enhance the understanding of people. The foundation tool is inexpensive and creates a basis for all other approaches – so it's like a building blocks. Common language, common structure.
https://luminalearning.com/
^{xx} **Harvard Business Review "What to do when you realize you made a bad hire.**
This 2018 article is a solid piece on dealing with a misjudged hire. It contains some eye-opening statistics on how often this occurs, and some additional underlying challenges that were brought out in the study shown in the next end note.
https://hbr.org/2018/08/what-to-do-when-you-realize-you-made-a-bad-hire
^{xxi} **Why New Hires Fail**
Leadership IQ, a Mark Murphy company carried out research for the book "Hiring for Attitude" in 2011. However, they updated this data and combined it with a new study in 2020 to provide some extremely revealing information about the impact of bad hiring.
https://www.leadershipiq.com/blogs/leadershipiq/35354241-why-new-hires-fail-emotional-intelligence-vs-skills
^{xxii} **Value Reporting Foundation**
This body is now folded in under the IASB and is part of the International Sustainability Standards Board. However, the integrated thinking and reporting framework remains a valid model.
https://www.valuereportingfoundation.org/
^{xxiii} **ISSB International Sustainability Standards Board**
Watch this space. At the moment the new board is in the early stages of consultation on how to move forward. While ISSB is a global organization (as is its' parent the IASF / IASB), there is also a European initiative called EFRAG that has already developed and issued requirements.
https://www.ifrs.org/groups/international-sustainability-standards-board/
^{xxiv} **Purpose of the Corporation**
It is worth a read of the press release of the original statement – there is also additional "one year ahead" information about progress.
https://www.businessroundtable.org/business-roundtable-redefines-the-purpose-of-a-corporation-to-promote-an-economy-that-serves-all-americans
^{xxv} **Harvard paper on Business Round Table statement on "Purpose"**

Research behind the paper entitled "The Illusory Promise of Stakeholder Governance" authored by Lucian A. Bebchuk and Roberto Tallarita, suggests that the statement about stakeholder primacy have not resulted in the anticipated changes. This was a contentious paper, strongly opposed by the BRT, but includes several facts that might lead one to be sceptical about the real desire for change.
https://papers.ssrn.com/sol3/papers.cfm?abstract_id=3544978

Manufactured by Amazon.ca
Bolton, ON

29323730R00092